William Hayley

Poems and Plays

William Hayley

Poems and Plays

ISBN/EAN: 9783744710084

Printed in Europe, USA, Canada, Australia, Japan

Cover: Foto ©Thomas Meinert / pixelio.de

More available books at **www.hansebooks.com**

POEMS

AND

PLAYS,

By WILLIAM HAYLEY, Esq.

IN SIX VOLUMES.

A NEW EDITION.

VOL. IV.

NOTES

TO THE

THIRD, FOURTH, and FIFTH EPISTLES

OF AN

ESSAY

ON

EPIC POETRY.

NOTES

TO THE

THIRD EPISTLE.

NOTE I. VERSE 36.

AND smiles of triumph hid his mortal pang.] An allusion to *ridens moriar*, the close of the celebrated Northern Ode, by the Danish king Regner Lodbrog; a translation of which is inserted in the curious little volume of Runic poetry, printed for Dodsley, 1763.

Bartholin, in his admirable Essay on the Causes which inspired the Danes with a Contempt of Death, affirms, that it was customary with the

Northern warriors to sing their own exploits in the close of life. He mentions the example of a hero, named Hallmundus, who being mortally wounded, commanded his daughter to attend while he composed a poem, and to inscribe it on a tablet of wood. BARTHOLIN. Lib. i. cap. 10.

NOTE II. VERSE 60.

And galls the ghostly tyrant with her lash.] The poetry of Provence contains many spirited satires against the enormities of the Clergy. The most remarkable, is the bold invective of the Troubadour Guillaume Figueira, in which he execrates the avarice and the cruelty of Rome. The Papal cause found a female Poet to defend it: Germonda of Montpellier composed a poetical reply to the satire of Figueira. See MILLOT's Hist. des Troubadours, vol. ii. p. 455.

NOTE III. VERSE 76.

Struck with ill-fated zeal the Latian lyre.] There never was a century utterly destitute of ingenious and elegant Poets, says the learned Polycarp Leiser, after having patiently traced the obscure progress of Latin poetry through all the dark

THIRD EPISTLE.

dark ages. Indeed the merit of some Latin Poets, in a period that we commonly suppose involved in the grossest barbarism, is singularly striking; many of these are of the Epic kind, and, as they describe the manners and customs of their respective times, a complete review of them might form a curious and entertaining work. I shall briefly mention such as appear most worthy of notice.

Abbo, a Parisian monk, of the Benedictine order, wrote a poem on the siege of Paris by the Normans and the Danes, at which he was present, in the year 886: it is printed in the second volume of Duchesne's Script. Francorum; and, though it has little or no poetical merit, may be regarded as an historical curiosity. The following lines, addressed to the city of Paris, in the beginning of the work, may serve as a specimen of its language:

> Dic igitur, præpulchra polis, quod Danea munus
> Libavit tibimet, soboles Plutonis amica,
> Tempore quo præsul domini et dulcissimus heros
> Gozlinus temet pastorque benignus alebat!
> Hæc, inquit, miror, narrare potest aliquisne?
> Nonne tuis idem vidisti oculis? refer ergo:
> Vidi equidem, jussisque tuis parebo libenter.

Leiser has confounded this Poet with another of this name; but Fabricius has corrected the mistake,

miftake, in his Bibliotheca Latina mediæ et infi-
mæ Ætatis.

Guido, Bifhop of Amiens from the year 1058
to 1076, wrote an Heroic poem on the exploits of
William the Conqueror, in which, according to
Ordericus Vitalis, he imitated both Virgil and
Statius. William of Apulia compofed, at the requeft of Pope Urban the IId, a poem, in five
books, on the actions of the Normans in Sicily,
Apulia, and Calabria, to the death of Robert
Guifcard their prince; addreffing his work to
the fon of that hero. It was written between the
years 1080 and 1099; firft printed in 1582, 4to;
and again in Muratori's Script. Ital.—Du Cange, in
his Notes to the Alexiad of the Princefs Anna
Comnena, has illuftrated that hiftory by frequent
and long quotations from William of Apulia; but
though the learned Critic gives him the title of
Scriptor Egregius, his poetry appears to me but a
few degrees fuperior to that of the Monk Abbo,
whom I have juft mentioned. The Reader may
judge from the following paffage, which I felect
not only as a fpecimen of the Author's ftyle, but
as it fhews that the wives of thefe martial Princes
fhared with them in all the perils of war:

Uxor

THIRD EPISTLE.

Uxor in hoc bello Roberti fortè fagittâ
Quâdam læfa fuit, quæ vulnere territa, nullam
Dum fperabat opem, fe penè fubegerat hofti,
Navigio cujus fe commendare volebat,
Inftantis metuens vicina pericula lethi:
Hanc deus eripuit, fieri ludibria nolens
Matronæ tantæ tam nobilis et venerandæ.

The Princefs Comnena has alfo celebrated the fortitude which this Heroine, whofe name was Gaita, difplayed in the battle; and it is remarkable that the royal female Hiftorian defcribes the noble Amazon more poetically than the Latin Poet.

Gualfredo, an Italian, who fucceeded to the bifhoprick of Siena in the year 1080, and died in 1127, wrote an Heroic poem on the expedition of Godfrey of Boulogne, which is faid to be ftill preferved in MS. at Siena. I believe Gualfredo is the firft Poet, in point of time, who treated of the happy fubject of the Crufades; which was afterwards embellifhed by two very elegant writers of Latin verfe, Ifcanus and Gunther, of whom I fhall prefently fpeak, and at length received its higheft honour from the genius of Taffo. There is alfo an early Latin poem on this fubject, the joint production of two writers, named Fulco and Ægidius, whom the accurate Fabricius places in the

beginning

beginning of the 13th century: the title of the work is Hiftoria Geftorum Viæ noftri Temporis Hierofolymitanæ. It is printed in the fourth volume of Duchefne's Script. Franc. and with confiderable additions in the third volume of Anecdota Edmundi Martene. I tranfcribe part of the opening of this poem, as the curious reader may have a pleafure in comparing it with that of Taffo:

> Ardor ineft, inquam, fententia fixaque menti
> Verfibus et numeris tranfmittere pofteritati
> Qualiter inftinctu deitatis, et aufpice cultu
> Eft aggreffa via memorando nobilis actu,
> Qua facrofancti violantes jura fepulchri
> Digna receperunt meriti commercia pravi.
> Inque fuis Truncis antiqua refurgere Troja
> Cœpit, et edomuit Chrifto contraria regna.

I will only add the portrait of Godfrey:

> Inclytus ille ducum Godefridus culmen honofque,
> Omnibus exemplum bonitatis militiæque,
> Sive hafta jaculans æquaret Parthica tela,
> Cominus aut feriens terebraret ferrea fcuta,
> Seu gladio pugnans carnes refecaret et offa,
> Sive eques atque pedes propelleret agmina denfa,
> Hic

THIRD EPISTLE.

Hic inimicitiis cunctis sibi conciliatis
Cunctis possessis pro Christi pace relictis
Arripuit callem Christum sectando vocantem.

The poem closes with the capture of Jerusalem.

Laurentius of Verona, who flourished about the year 1120, wrote an Heroic poem, in seven books, intitled, Rerum in Majorica Pisanorum. Edidit Ughellus, tom. 3. Italiæ sacræ.

But, in merit and reputation, these early Latin Poets of modern time are very far inferior to Philip Gualtier de Chatillon, who seems to have been the first that caught any portion of true poetic spirit in Latin verse. He was Provost of the Canons of Tournay * about the year 1200, according to Mr. Warton, who has given some specimens of his style in the second Dissertation prefixed to his admirable History of English Poetry. I shall therefore only add, that the best edition of his Alexandreid, an Heroic poem in ten books on Alexander the Great, was printed at Leyden, 4to, 1558.

The superior merit of Josephus Iscanus, or

* Fabricius calls him Episcopus Magalonensis. Bib. Lat. tom. ii. p. 255.

Joseph of Exeter, has been also displayed by the same judicious Encomiast, in the Dissertation I have mentioned; nor has he failed to commemorate two Latin Epic Poets of the same period, and of considerable merit for the time in which they lived—Gunther, and. William of Bretagny: the first was a German monk, who wrote after the year 1108, and has left various historical and poetical works; particularly two of the Epic kind —Solymarium, a poem on the taking of Jerusalem by Godfrey of Bulloign; and another, intitled Ligurinus, on the exploits of the Emperor Frederick Barbarossa, which he compleated during the life of that Prince. The first was never printed; of the latter there have been several editions, and one by the celebrated Melancthon, in 1569. That his poetical merit was considerable in many respects, will appear from the following verses, in which he speaks of himself;

Hoc quoque me famæ, si desint cætera, solum
Conciliare potest, quod jam per multa latentes
Sæcula, nec clausis prodire penatibus ausas
Picrides vulgare paro, priscumque nitorem
Reddere carminibus, tardosque citare poetas.

William

THIRD EPISTLE.

William of Bretagny was preceptor to Pierre Charlot, natural fon of Philip Auguftus, King of France, and addreffed a poem to his pupil, intitled Karlotis, which is yet unpublifhed; but his greater work, called Philippis, an Heroic poem in twelve books, is printed in the collections of Duchefne and Pithæus; and in a feparate 4to volume, with a copious commentary by Barthius. Notwithftanding the praifes beftowed on this Author by his learned Commentator, who prefers him to all his contemporaries, he appears to me inferior in poetic fpirit to his three rivals, Gualtier de Chatillon, Ifcanus, and Gunther. Yet his work is by no means defpicable in its ftyle, and may be confidered as a valuable picture of the times in which he lived; for he was himfelf engaged in many of the fcenes which he defcribes. His profeft defign is to celebrate the exploits of Philip Auguftus; and he clofes his poem with the death of that Monarch, which happened in 1223. He addreffes his work, in two feparate poetical dedications, to Lewis, the fucceffor of Philip, and to Pierre Charlot his natural fon, who was Bifhop of Noyon in 1240, and died 1249. He feems to have been excited to this compofition by the reputation of Gualtier's Alexandreid; to which he thus alludes, in the verfes addreffed to Lewis:

Gefta

Gesta ducis Macedum celebri describere versu
Si licuit, Gualtere, tibi, quæ sola relatu
Multivago docuit te vociferatio famæ —

— — — — —

Cur ego quæ novi, proprio quæ lumine vidi,
Non ausim magni magnalia scribere regis,
Qui nec Alexandro minor est virtute, nec illo
Urbi Romuleæ totum qui subdidit orbem?

He takes occasion also, in two other parts of his poem, to pay a liberal compliment to Gualtier, to whom, in poetical ability, he confesses himself inferior; but this inferiority his admirer Barthius will not allow. Of their respective talents the reader may judge, who will compare the passage which Mr. Warton has cited from the Alexandreid, with the following lines, in which William of Bretagny uses the very simile of his predecessor, comparing his hero Philip to a young lion;

Rex dolet ereptum comitem sibi, frendit, et iræ
Occultare nequit tectos sub pectore motus,
Nam rubor in vultu duplicatus prodit apertè
Quam gravis illustrem trahit indignatio mentem.
Qualiter in Lybicis spumante leunculo rictu
Saltibus ungue ferox, et dentibus asper aduncis,

Fortis

Fortis et horrisonis anno jam penè secundo,
Cui venatoris venabula forte per armos
Descendere levi stringentia vulnere corpus,
Colla rigens hirsuta jubis desævit in hostem
Jam retrocedentem, nec eum tetigisse volentem,
Cum nihil ex facto referat nisi dedecus illo.
Nec mora nec requies, quin jam deglutiat ipsum,
Ni prudens hostis prætenta cuspide scuto
Unguibus objecto, dum dat vestigia retro,
In loca se retrahat non irrumpenda leoni.
Sic puer in comitem rex debacchatur, et ipsum
Subsequitur presso relegens vestigia gressu.

I will add the following passage from the eleventh Book, as it contains an animated portrait, and a simile more original than the preceding.

At lævo in cornu, qui nulli marte secundus,
Bolonides pugnæ insistit, cui fraxinus ingens
Nunc implet dextram, vix ulli bajula, qualem
In Bacchi legimus portasse Capanea cunas,
Quam vix fulmineo dejecit Jupiter ictu;
Nunc culter vitæ impatiens, nunc sanguine pugni
Mucro rubens; gemina e sublimi vertice fulgens
Cornua conus agit, superasque eduxit in auras
E costis assumpta nigris, quas faucis in antro
Branchia balenæ Britici colit incola ponti;

Ut

Ut qui magnus erat magnæ fuperaddita moli
Majorem faceret phantaſtica pompa videri;
Ac velut in ſaltus ſcopuloſa Bieria ſaltu
Præcipiti mittit ingenti corpore cervum,
Cujus multifidos numerant a cornibus annos,
Menſe ſub Octobri nondum Septembre peracto,
Annua quandò novis Venus incitat ignibus illum,
Curſitat in cervos ramoſa fronte minores,
Omnibus ut pulſis victor ſub tegmine fagi
Connubio cervam ſolus ſibi ſubdat amatam.
Haud ſecus e peditum medio, quibus ipſe rotundo
Ut caſtro cauta ſe circumſepſerat arte,
Proſiliens volat in Thomam, Robertigenaſque
Drocarum Comitem; Belvacenumque Philippum
Bolonides.———

William of Bretagny had an immediate ſucceſſor in Latin poetry, who appears to have at leaſt an equal portion of poetical ſpirit; the name of this Author is Nicholas de Brai, who wrote an Heroic poem on the actions of Louis the VIIIth, after the death of that Monarch, and addreſſed it to William of Auvergne, who was Biſhop of Paris from the year 1228 to 1248. As a ſpecimen of his deſcriptive power, I ſelect the following lines, which form part of a long deſcription of a Goblet preſented to the King on his acceſſion:

———Parant

———Parant intrare palatia regis
Magnifici cives, gratiffima dona ferentes,
Tegmina quos ornant variis infculpta figuris;
Et patrem patriæ jucunda voce falutant,
Et genibus flexis præfentant ditia dona.

Offertur crater, quem fi fit credere dignum.
Perditus ingenio fabricavit Mulciber auro;
Margine crateris totus depingitur orbis,
Et feries rerum brevibus diftincta figuris;
Illic pontus erat, tellus, et pendulus aer,
Ignis ad alta volans cœli fupereminet illis:
Quatuor in partes orbis diftinguitur, ingens
Circuit oceanus immenfis fluctibus orbem.
Ingenio natura fuo duo lumina fecit
Fixa tenore poli, mundi famulantia rebus.

The Author proceeds to defcribe Thebes and Troy, as they are figured on this fuperb Goblet; and concludes his account of the workmanfhip with the four following lines, of peculiar beauty for the age in which they appeared:

Martis adulterium refupino margine pinxit
Mulciber, et Venerem laqueis cum Marte ligavit;
Pluraque cælaffet fub margine, fed pudor illi
Obftat, et ingentis renovatur caufa doloris.

This

This Poem, which the author seems to have left imperfect, is printed in the fifth volume of Duchesne's Script: Francorum:—England is said to have produced another Heroic Poet of considerable merit, who celebrated in Latin verse the exploits of Richard the First, and who was called Gulielmus Peregrinus, from his having attended that Prince to the Holy Land. Leland mentions him by the name of Gulielmus de Canno, and Pits calls him Poetarum sui temporis apud nostrates facile Princeps; but I do not find that his Work was ever printed; nor do the several biographical writers who speak of him, inform us where it exists in MS.

In Italy the Latin language is supposed to have been cultivated with still greater success, and the restoration of its purity is in great measure ascribed to Albertino Mussato, whose merits were first displayed to our country by the learned author of the Essay on Pope:—Mussato was a Paduan, of high rank and great talents, but unfortunate. He died in exile, 1329, and left, besides many smaller Latin pieces, an Heroic Poem; De Gestis Italorum post Henricum VII. Cæsarem; seu de Obsidione Domini Canis Grandis de Verona circa Mœnia Paduanæ Civitatis et Conflictu ejus:—Quadrio, from whom I transcribe this title, says it is printed

in

in the tenth volume of Muratori. Voffius, who speaks of him as an Hiftorian, afferts that he commanded in the war which is the fubject of his Poem.

In a few years after the death of Muffato, Petrarch received the laurel at Rome, for his Latin Epic poem, intitled Africa; a performance which has funk fo remarkably from the high reputation it once obtained, that the great admirer and encomiaft of Petrarch, who has publifhed three entertaining quarto volumes on his life, calls it " Un ouvrage fans chaleur, fans invention, fans interet, qui n'a pas meme le merite de la verfification & du ftyle, & dont il eft impoffible de foutenir la lecture.—I muft obferve, however, that Taffo, in his Effay on Epic Poetry, beftows a very high encomium on that part of Petrarch's Latin poem, in which he celebrates the loves of Sophonifba and Mafiniffa; and indeed the cenfure of this amiable French writer, who in other points has done ample juftice to the merits of Petrarch, appears to me infinitely too fevere. There are many paffages in this neglected Poem conceived with great force and imagination, and expreffed with equal elegance of language. I fhall felect fome verfes from that part of it which has been honoured by the applaufe of Taffo. The following

VOL. IV.   C

following lines describe the anguish of the young Numidian Prince, when he is constrained to abandon his lovely bride:

Volvitur inde thoro (quoniam sub pectore pernox
Sævit amor, lacerantque truces præcordia curæ),
Uritur, invigilant mœror, metus, ira, furorque;
Sæpè & abfentem lacrymans dum ftringit amicam,
Sæpè thoro dedit amplexus et dulcia verba.
Poftquam nulla valent violento fræna dolori,
Incipit, et longis folatur damna querelis:
Cura mihi nimium, vita mihi dulcior omni,
Sophonifba, vale! non te, mea cura, videbo
Leniter æthereos pofthac componere vultus,
Effufofque auro religantem ex more capillos;
Dulcia non cœlum mulcentia verba Deofque
Oris odorati, fecretaque murmura, carpam.
Solus ero, gelidoque infternam membra cubili;
Atque utinam focio componat amica fepulchro,
Et fimul hic vetitos, illic concorditer annos,
Contingat duxiffe mihi fors optima bufti.
Si cinis amborum commixtis morte medullis
Unus erit, Scipio noftros non fcindet amores.
O utinam infernis etiam nunc una latebris
Umbra fimus, liceat pariter per clauftra vagari
Myrtea, nec noftros Scipio disjungat amores.
Ibimus una ambo flentes, et paffibus iifdem
          Ibimus,

Ibimus, æterno connexi fœdere ; nec nos
Ferreus aut æquos Scipio interrumpet amores.

The well-known cataſtrophe of the unfortunate Sophoniſba is related with much poetical ſpirit. The cloſe of her life, and her firſt appearance in the regions of the dead, are peculiarly ſtriking:

Illa manu pateramque tenens, & lumina cœlo
Attollens, Sol alme, inquit, Superique valete!
Maſiniſſa, vale! noſtri memor; inde malignum
Ceu ſitiens haurit non mota fronte venenum,
Tartareaſque petit violentus ſpiritus umbras.

Nulla magis Stygios mirantum obſeſſa corona
Umbra lacus ſubiit, poſtquam diviſa triformis
Partibus haud æquis ſtetit ingens machina mundi.
Obtutu attonito ſtabant horrentia circum
Agmina Pœnarum, ſparſoque rigentia villo
Eumenidum tacitis inhiabant rictibus ora.
Regia vis oculis inerat, pallorque verendus,
Et vetus egregia majeſtas fronte manebat.
Indignata tamen ſuperis, irataque morti,
Ibat et exiguo deſigens lumina flexu.

With Petrarch I may cloſe this curſory review of the neglected authors who wrote Heroic peoms in Latin, during the courſe of the dark ages.—A peculiar circumſtance induces me to add another name to the preceding liſt. John, Abbot of Peterborough, in the reign of Edward the Third, wrote an Heroic poem, intitled Bellum Navarrenſe, 1366, de Petro rege Aragoniæ & Edwardo Principe. This performance, containing five hundred and ſixty verſes, is ſaid to be preſerved in MS. in the Bodleian Library; and I have thought it worthy of notice, becauſe it treats of the very ſubject on whch Dryden informs us he had once projected an Epic poem.

Of the many Latin compoſitions of the Epic kind, which later times have produced, the Chriſtiad of Vida, the Sarcotis of Maſſenius, and the Conſtantine of Mambrun, appear to me the moſt worthy of regard; but even theſe are ſeldom peruſed: and indeed the Poet, who in a poliſhed age prefers the uſe of a dead language to that of a living one, can only expect, and perhaps only deſerves, the attention of a few curious ſequeſtered ſtudents.

NOTE IV. Verse 81.

Thy daring Dante his wild viſion ſung.] Dante Allighieri was born at Florence, in May 1265, of

an

THIRD EPISTLE. 21

an ancient and honourable family. Boccacio, who lived in the same peirod, has left a very curious and entertaining Treatise, on the Life, the Studies, and Manners of this extraordinary Poet; whom he regarded as his master, and for whose memory he professed the highest veneration. This interesting biographer relates, that Dante, before he was nine years old, conceived a passion for the lady whom he has immortalized in his singular Poem. Her age was near his own; and her name was Beatrice, the daughter of Folco Portinari, a noble citizen of Florence. Of this fair one the best accounts are obscure. Some refining commentators have even denied her corporeal existence; affirming her to be nothing more or less than Theology: but we may question if Theology was ever the mistress of so young a lover. The passion of Dante, however, like that of his successor Petrarch, seems to have been of the chaste and Platonic kind, according to the account he has himself given of it, in one of his early productions, intitled Vita Nuova; a mixture of mysterious poetry and prose, in which he mentions both the origin of his affection, and the death of his mistress; who, according to Boccacio, died at the age of twenty-four. The same author asserts, that Dante fell into a deep melancholy in consequence of this event,

event, from which his friends endeavoured to raife him, by perfuading him to marriage. After fome time he followed their advice, and repented it; for he unfortunately made choice of a lady who bore fome refemblance to the celebrated Xantippe. The Poet, not poffeffing the patience of Socrates, feparated himfelf from her with fuch vehement expreffions of diflike, that he never afterwards admitted her to his prefence, though fhe had borne him feveral children.—In the early part of his life he gained fome credit in a military character; diftinguifhing himfelf by his bravery in an action where the Florentines obtained a fignal victory over the citizens of Arezzo. He became ftill more eminent by the acquifition of civil honours; and at the age of thirty-five he rofe to be one of the chief magiftrates of Florence, when that dignity was conferred by the fuffrages of the people. From this exaltation the Poet himfelf dated his principal misfortunes, as appears from the fragment of a letter quoted by Lionardo Bruni, one of his early biographers, where Dante fpeaks of his political failure with that liberal franknefs which integrity infpires.—Italy was at that time diftracted by the contending factions of the Ghibellins and the Guelphs: the latter, among whom Dante took an active part, were again divided into the Blacks and

and the Whites. Dante, says Gravina, exerted all his influence to unite these inferior parties; but his efforts were ineffectual, and he had the misfortune to be unjustly persecuted by those of his own faction. A powerful citizen of Florence, named Corso Donati, had taken measures to terminate these intestine broils, by introducing Charles of Valois, brother to Philip the Fair, King of France. Dante, with great vehemence, opposed this disgraceful project, and obtained the banishment of Donati and his partizans. The exiles applied to the Pope (Boniface the VIIIth), and by his assistance succeeded in their design. Charles of Valois entered Florence in triumph, and those who had opposed his admission were banished in their turn. Dante had been dispatched to Rome as the ambassador of his party, and was returning, when he received intelligence of the revolution in his native city. His enemies, availing themselves of his absence, had procured an iniquitous sentence against him, by which he was condemned to banishment, and his possessions were confiscated. His two enthusiastic biographers, Boccacio and Manetti, express the warmest indignation against this injustice of his country.—Dante, on receiving the intelligence, took refuge in Siena, and afterwards in Arezzo, where many of his party were assembled.

An attempt was made to furprife the city of Florence, by a fmall army which Dante is fuppofed to have attended; the defign mifcarried, and our Poet is conjectured to have wandered to various parts of Italy, till he found a patron in the great Can della Scala, Prince of Verona, whom he has celebrated in his Poem. The high fpirit of Dante was ill fuited to courtly dependence; and he is faid to have loft the favour of his Veronefe patron by the rough franknefs of his behaviour. From Verona he retired to France, according to Manetti; and Boccacio affirms that he difputed in the Theological Schools of Paris with great reputation. Bayle queftions his vifiting Paris at this period of his life, and thinks it improbable that a man, who had been one of the chief magiftrates of Florence, fhould condefcend to engage in the public fquabbles of the Parifian Theologifts. But the fpirit both of Dante, and the times in which he lived, fufficiently account for this exercife of his talents; and his refidence in France at this feafon is confirmed by Boccacio, in his life of our Poet, which Bayle feems to have had no opportunity of confulting.

 The election of Henry Count of Luxemburgh to the empire, in November 1308, afforded Dante a profpect of being reftored to his native city, as he attached himfelf to the intereft of the new Em

†   peror,

peror, in whose service he is supposed to have written his Latin treatise De Monarchia, in which he asserted the rights of the Empire against the encroachments of the Papacy. In the year 1311, he instigated Henry to lay siege to Florence; in which enterprize, says one of his Biographers, he did not appear in person, from motives of respect towards his native city. The Emperor was repulsed by the Florentines; and his death, which happened in the succeeding year, deprived Dante of all hopes concerning his re-establishment in Florence.

After this disappointment, he is supposed to have passed some years in roving about Italy in a state of poverty and distress, till he found an honourable establishment at Ravenna, under the protection of Guido Novello da Polenta, the lord of that city, who received this illustrious exile with the most endearing liberality, continued to protect him through the few remaining years of his life, and extended his munificence to the ashes of the Poet.

Eloquence was one of the many talents which Dante possessed in an eminent degree. On this account he is said to have been employed on fourteen different embassies in the course of his life, and to have succeeded in most of them. His patron Guido had occasion to try his abilities in a service of this

nature,

nature, and dispatched him as his ambassador to negociate a peace with the Venetians, who were preparing for hostilities against Ravenna. Manetti asserts that he was unable to procure a public audience at Venice, and returned to Ravenna by land, from his apprehensions of the Venetian fleet; when the fatigue of his journey, and the mortification of failing in his attempt to preserve his generous patron from the impending danger, threw him into a fever, which terminated in death on the 14th of September 1321. He died, however, in the palace of his friend, and the affectionate Guido paid the most tender regard to his memory. This magnificent patron, says Boccacio, commanded the body to be adorned with poetical ornaments, and, after being carried on a bier through the streets of Ravenna by the most illustrious citizens, to be deposited in a marble coffin. He pronounced himself the funeral oration, and expressed his design of erecting a splendid monument in honour of the deceased: a design which his subsequent misfortunes rendered him unable to accomplish. At his request, many epitaphs were written on the Poet: the best of them, says Boccacio, by Giovanni del Virgilio of Bologna, a famous author of that time, and the intimate friend of Dante. Boccacio then cites a few Latin verses, not
worth

THIRD EPISTLE.

worth tranfcribing, fix of which are quoted by Bayle as the compofition of Dante himfelf, on the authority of Paul Jovius. In 1483, Bernardo Bembo, the father of the celebrated Cardinal, raifed a handfome monument over the neglected afhes of the Poet, with the following infcription:

Exigua tumuli Danthes hic forte jacebas
   Squallenti nulli cognita pæne fitu;
At nunc marmoreo fubnixus conderis arcu,
   Omnibus et cultu fplendidiore nites:
Nimirum Bembus, Mufis incenfus Etrufcis,
   Hoc tibi, quem in primis hæ coluere, dedit.

Before this period the Florentines had vainly endeavoured to obtain the bones of their great Poet from the city of Ravenna. In the age of Leo the Xth they made a fecond attempt, by a folemn application to the Pope for that purpofe; and the great Michael Angelo, an enthufiaftic admirer of Dante, very liberally offered to execute a magnificent monument to the Poet. The hopes of the Florentines were again unfuccefsful. The particulars of their fingular petition may be found in the notes to Condivi's Life of Michael Angelo.

The perfon and manners of Dante are thus reprefented by the defcriptive pen of Boccacio:—

" Fu

" Fu adunque questo nostro Poeta di Mezzana
statura; e poichè alla matura età fu pervenuto,
andò alquanto gravetto, ed era il suo andar grave,
e mansueto, di onestissimi panni sempre vestito, in
quello abito, che era alla sua matura età convene-
vole; il suo volto fu lungo, il naso aquilino, gli
occhi anzi grossi, che piccioli, le mascelle grandi,
e dal labbro di sotto, era quel di sopra avanzato; il
colore era bruno, i capelli, e la barba spessi neri e
crespi,

A GUIDO CAVALCANTI.

 Guido, vorrei, che tu, e Lappo, ed io,
  Fossimo presi per incantamento,
  E messi ad un vassel, ch'ad ogni vento
  Per mare andasse a voler vostro e mio;
 Sicché fortuna, od altro tempo rio,
  Non ci potesse dare impedimento:
  Anzi vivendo sempre in noi talento
  Di stare insieme crescesse 'l disio.
 E monna Vanna, e monna Bice poi,
  Con quella su il numer delle trenta,
  Con noi ponesse il buono incantatore:
  E quivi ragionar sempre d' amore:
  E ciascuna di lor fosse contenta,
  Siccome io credo che sariamo noi.

I M I.

crespi, e sempre nella faccia malinconico e pensoso
——Ne costumi publici e domestici mirabilmente
fu composto e ordinato; più che niuno altro cortese
e civile; nel cibo e nel poto fu modestissimo.——
Though Dante is described as much inclined to
melancholy, and his genius particularly delighted
in the gloomy and sublime, yet in his early period
of life he seems to have possessed all the lighter
graces of sprightly composition, as appears from
the following airy and sportive sonnet:

IMITATION.

Henry! I wish that you, and Charles, and I,
   By some sweet spell within a bark were plac'd,
   A gallant bark with magic virtue grac'd,
   Swift at our will with every wind to fly:
So that no changes of the shifting sky,
   No stormy terrors of the watery waste,
   Might bar our course, but heighten still our taste
Of sprightly joy, and of our social tie:
Then, that my Lucy, Lucy fair and free,
   With those soft nymphs on whom your souls
      are bent,
The kind magician might to us convey,
To talk of love throughout the live-long day;
   And that each fair might be as well content
   As I in truth believe our hearts would be.

                                  These

These lively verses were evidently written before the Poet lost the object of his earliest attachment, as she is mentioned by the name of Bice. At what time, and in what place, he executed the great and singular work which has rendered him immortal, his numerous Commentators seem unable to determine. Boccacio asserts, that he began it in his thirty-fifth year, and had finished seven Cantos of his Inferno before his exile; that in the plunder of his house, on that event, the beginning of his poem was fortunately preserved, but remained for some time neglected; till its merit being accidentally discovered by an intelligent Poet, named Dino, it was sent to the Marquis Maroello Malespina, an Italian nobleman, by whom Dante was then protected. The Marquis restored these lost papers to the Poet, and entreated him to proceed in a work which opened in so promising a manner. To this incident we are probably indebted for the poem of Dante, which he must have continued under all the disadvantages of an unfortunate and agitated life. It does not appear at what time he completed it; perhaps before he quitted Verona, as he dedicated the Paradise to his Veronese patron.——The Critics have variously accounted for his having called his poem Comedia. He gave it that title, said one of his sons, because it opens with distress, and closes with felicity. The very high

estimation

estimation in which this production was held by his country, appears from a singular institution. The republic of Florence, in the year 1373, assigned a public stipend to a person appointed to read lectures on the poem of Dante: Boccacio was the first person engaged in this office; but his death happening in two years after his appointment, his Comment extended only to the seventeen first Cantos of the Inferno. The critical dissertations that have been written on Dante are almost as numerous as those to which Homer has given birth: the Italian, like the Grecian Bard, has been the subject of the highest panegyric, and of the grossest invective. Voltaire has spoken of him with that precipitate vivacity, which so frequently led that lively Frenchman to insult the reputation of the noblest writers. In one of his entertaining letters, he says to an Italian Abbé, " Je fais grand cas du courage, avec lequel vous avez osé dire que Dante etoit un fou, et son ouvrage un monstre — — — Le Dante pourra entrer dans les bibliotheques des curieux, mais il ne sera jamais lu." But more temperate and candid Critics have not been wanting, to display the merits of this original Poet. Mr. Warton has introduced into his last volume on English Poetry, a judicious and spirited summary of Dante's performance. We have

have several versions of the celebrated story of Ugolino; but I believe no entire Canto of Dante has hitherto appeared in our language, though his whole work has been translated into French, Spanish, and Latin verse. The three Cantos which follow were translated a few years ago, to oblige a particular friend. The Author has since been solicited to execute an entire translation of Dante: but the extreme inequality of this Poet would render such a work a very laborious undertaking; and it appears very doubtful how far such a version would interest our country. Perhaps the reception of these Cantos may discover to
the

DELL' INFERNO.

CANTO I.

NEL mezzo del cammin di nostra vita
 Mi ritrovai per una selva oscura,
 Che la diritta via era smarrita:
E quanto à dir qual era, è cosa dura,
 Questa selva selvaggia ed aspra e forte,
 Che nel pensier rinnuova la paura.

Tanto

the Tranflator the fentiments of the public. At all events, he flatters himfelf that the enfuing portion of a celebrated poem may afford fome pleafure from its novelty, as he has endeavoured to give the Englifh reader an idea of Dante's peculiar manner, by adopting his triple rhyme; and he does not recollect that this mode of verfification has ever appeared before in our language: it has obliged him, of courfe, to make the number of tranflated lines correfpond exactly with thofe of the original. The difficulties attending this metre will fufficiently fhew themfelves, and obtain fome degree of indulgence from the intelligent and candid reader.

THE INFERNO OF DANTE.

CANTO I.

IN the mid feafon of this mortal ftrife,
   I found myfelf within a gloomy grove,
Far wandering from the ways of perfect life:
The place I know not, where I chanc'd to rove;
   It was a wood fo wild, it wounds me fore
   But to remember with what ills I ftrove:

Such

Tanto è amara, che poco è più morte:
  Ma per trattar del ben, ch'i vi trovai,
  Dirò dell' altre cofe, ch'i v'ho fcorte.
I non fo ben ridir, com'i v'entrai;
  Tant'era pien di fonno in fu quel punto,
  Che la verace via abbandonai.
Ma po' ch'i fui al piè d'un colle giunto,
  Là ove terminava quella valle,
  Che m'avea di paura il cor compunto;
Guarda'in alto, e vidi le fue fpalle
  Veftite già de' raggi del pianeta,
  Che mena dritto altrui per ogni calle.
Allor fu la paura un poco queta,
  Che nel lago del cor m'era durata,
  La notte, ch'i paffai con tanta pieta.
E come quei, che con lena affannata
  Ufcito fuor del pelago alla riva,
  Si volge all'aqua perigliofa, e guata;
Cofi l'animo mio, ch'ancor fuggiva,
  Si vols' à retro à rimirar lo paffo,
  Che non lafciò giammai perfona viva.
Poi ch'ebbi ripofato il corpo laffo,
  Riprefi via per la piaggia deferta,
  Si che 'l piè fermo fempre era 'l più baffo.
Ed ecco, quafi al cominciar dell' erta,
  Una lonza leggiera e prefta molto,
  Che di pel maculato era coperta.

E non

THIRD EPISTLE.

Such still my dread, that death is little more.
   But I will tell the good which there I found.
   High things 'twas there my fortune to explore:
Yet how I enter'd on that secret ground
   I know not to explain; so much in sleep
   My mortal senses at that hour were drown'd.
But when I reach'd the bottom of a steep,
   That rose to terminate the dreary vale,
   Which made cold terrors thro' my bosom creep,
I look'd on high, where breath'd a purer gale,
   And saw the summit glisten with that ray
   Which leads the wand'rer safe o'er hill and dale.
This soon began to chase those fears away,
   Which held my struggling spirit bound so fast
   During that night of darkness and dismay:
And, as th' exausted wretch, by fortune cast
   Safe from the stormy deep upon the shore,
   Turns to survey the perils he has past,
So turn'd my soul, ere yet its dread was o'er,
   Back to contemplate that mysterious strait
   Where living mortal never past before.
Arising soon from this repose elate,
   Up the rough steep my journey I begin,
   My lower foot sustaining all my weight.
Here, while my toilsome way I slowly win,
   Behold a nimble Panther springs to fight!
   And beauteous spots adorn his motley skin:

E non mi fi partia dinanzi al volto;
   Anz' impediva tanto 'l mio cammino,
   Ch'i fu per ritornar più volte volto.
Temp' era dal principio del mattino,
   E 'l fol montava in fu con quelle ftelle,
   Ch' eran con lui, quando l'amor divino
Moffe da prima quelle cofe belle
   Si ch'a bene fperar m'era cagione
   Di quella fera la gaietta pelle,
L'ora del tempo, e la dolce ftagione:
   Ma non fi, che paura non mi deffe
   La vifta, che m'apparve d'un leone.
Quefti parea, che contra me veneffe
   Con la teft'alta, e con rabbiofa fame,
   Si che parea, che l'aer ne temeffe:
Ed una lupa, che di tutte brame
   Sembiava carca con la fua magrezza,
   E molte genti fe' già viver grame.
Quefta mi porfe tanto di gravezza
   Con la paura, ch'ufcia di fua vifta,
   Ch'i perde' la fperanza dell' altezza.
E quale è quei, che volentieri acquifta,
   E gingne 'l tempo, che perder lo face,
   Che 'n tutt' i fuoi penfier piange, e s'attrifta;
Tal me fece la beftia fenza pace,
   Che venendomi 'ncontro, a poco a poco
   Mi ripingeva là, dove 'l fol tace.

Mentre

THIRD EPISTLE.

He at my prefence fhew'd no figns of fright,
  But rather ftrove to bar my doubtful way;
  I often turn'd, and oft refolv'd on flight.
'Twas now the chearful hour of rifing day;
  The fun advanc'd in that propitious fign
  Which firft beheld his radiant beams difplay
Creation's charms, the work of love divine!
  So that I now was rais'd to hope fublime,
  By thefe bright omens of a fate benign,
The beauteous Beaft and the fweet hour of prime.
  But foon I loft that hope; and fhook yet more
  To fee a Lion in this lonely clime:
With open jaws, athirft for human gore,
  He rufh'd towards me in his hungry ire;
  Air feem'd to tremble at his favage roar.
With him, enflam'd with every fierce defire,
  A famifh'd She-wolf, like a fpectre, came;
  Beneath whofe gripe fhall many a wretch expire.
Such fad oppreffion feiz'd my finking frame,
  Such horror at thefe ftrange tremendous fights,
  My hopes to climb the hill no longer aim;
But, as the wretch whom lucre's luft incites,
  In the curft hour which fcatters all his wealth,
  Sinks in deep forrow, dead to all delights,
So was I robb'd of all my fpirit's health,
  And to the quarter where the fun grows mute,
  Driven by this Beaft, who crept on me by ftealth.

Mentre cn'i rovinava in baſſo loco,
 Dinanzi gli occhi mi ſi fu offerto
 Chi per lungo ſilenzio parea fioco.
Quando i' vidi coſtui nel gran diſerto;
 Miſerere di me gridai a lui,
 Qual che tu ſii, od ombra, od uomo certo.
Riſpoſemi: non uomo, uomo già fui,
 E li parenti miei furon Lombardi,
 E Mantovani, per patria amendui.
Nacqui ſub Julio, ancorche foſſe tardi,
 E viſſi a Roma, ſotto 'l buono Aguſto,
 Al tempo degli Dei falſi e bugiardi.
Poeta fui, e cantai di quel giuſto
 Figlioul d'Anchiſe, che venne da Troja,
 Poichè 'l ſuperbo Ilion fu combuſto.
Ma tu, perchè ritorni à tanta noja?
 Perchè non ſali il dilettoſo monte,
 Ch'è principio e cagion di tutta gioja?
Or ſe' tu quel Virgilio, e quella fonte,
 Che ſpande di parlar sì largo fiume?
 Riſpoſi lui, con vergognoſa fronte.
Oh degli altri poeti onore e lume,
 Vagliami 'l lungo ſtudio, e 'l grande amore,
 Che m'han fatto cercar lo tuo volume.
Tu ſe' lo mio maeſtro, e 'l mio autore:
 Tu ſe' ſolo colui, da cu'io tolſi
 Lo bello ſtile, che m'ha fatto onore.

THIRD EPISTLE.

While I retreated from her dread purfuit,
   A manly figure my glad eyes furvey'd,
   Whofe voice was like the whifper of a lute.
Soon as I faw him in this dreary glade,
   Take pity on me, to this form I cry'd,
   Be thou fubftantial man, or fleeting fhade !—
A man I was (the gracious form reply'd)
   And both my parents were of Lombard race;
   They in their native Mantua liv'd and dy'd:
I liv'd at Rome, rich in a monarch's grace,
   Beneath the good Auguftus' letter'd reign,
   While fabled Gods were ferv'd with worfhip bafe.
A Bard I was: the fubject of my ftrain
   That juft and pious Chief who fail'd from Troy,
   Sinking in afhes on the fanguine plain.
But thou, whom thefe portentous fights annoy,
   Why doft thou turn? why not afcend the mount,
   Source of all good, and fummit of all joy!—
Art thou that Virgil? thou! that copious fount
   Of richeft eloquence, fo clear, fo bright?
   I anfwer'd, blufhing at his kind account;
O thou! of Poets the pure guide and light!
   Now let me profit by that fond efteem
   Which kept thy fong for ever in my fight!
Thou art my Mafter! thou my Bard fupreme,
   From whom alone my fond ambition drew
   That purer ftyle which I my glory deem!

'Vedi la beſtia, per cu'io mi volſi :
　Ajutami da lei, famoſo ſaggio,
　Ch'ella mi fa tremar le vene e i polſi,
A te convien tenere altro viaggio,
　Riſpoſe, poichè lagrimar mi vide,
　Se vuoi campar d'eſto luogo ſelvaggio:
Che queſta beſtia, per la qual tu gride,
　Non laſcia altrui paſſar per la ſua via,
　Ma tanto lo 'mpediſce, che l'uccide;
Ed ha natura sì malvagia e ria,
　Che mai non empie la bramoſa voglia,
　E, dopo 'l paſto, ha più fame, che pria.
Molti ſon gli animali, a cui s'ammoglia;
　E più ſaranno ancora, infin che 'l veltro
　Verrà, che la farà morir di doglia.
Queſti non ciberà terra, nè peltro,
　Ma ſapienza, e amore, e virtute,
　E ſua nazion ſarà tra Feltro e Feltro:
Di quell' umile Italia fia ſalute,
　Per cui morío la Vergine Cammilla,
　Eurialo, e Turno, e Niſo di ferute:
Queſti la caccerà per ogni villa,
　Fin chè l'avrà rimeſſa nello 'nferno,
　La onde 'nvidia prima dipartilla.
Ond' Io, per lo tuo me', penſo e diſcerno,
　Che tu mi ſegui, ed io ſarò tua guida,
　E trarrotti di qui, per luogo eterno,

　　　　　　　　　　　　　　　Ov'

THIRD EPISTLE.

O! from this Beast, so hideous to the view,
   Save me! O save me! thou much-honour'd Sage!
For growing terrors all my power subdue.—
A different road must lead thee from her rage,
   (He said, observant of my starting tears)
   And from this wild thy spirit disengage;
For that terrific Beast, which caus'd thy fears,
   Worries each wretch that in her road she spies,
   Till death at length, his sole relief, appears.
So keen her nature, sleep ne'er seals her eyes;
   Her ravenous hunger no repast can sate;
   Food only serves to make its fury rise.
She calls from different animals her mate;
   And long shall she produce an offspring base,
   Then from a mighty victor meet her fate.
Nor pomp nor riches shall that victor grace,
   But truth, and love, and all excelling worth;
   He from his rescu'd land all ill shall chase,
The saviour of the realm that gives him birth,
   Of Italy, for whom Camilla fell,
   And Turnus, fighting for his native earth,
And Nisus, with the friend he lov'd so well.
   The Beast this victor to that den shall drive
   Whence Envy let her loose, her native hell!
Now for thy good, well-pleas'd, I will contrive,
   That by my aid, while I thy steps controul,
   Thou shalt in safety at those realms arrive
                      Where

Ov' udirai le disperate strida,
  Vedrai gli antiche spiriti dolenti,
  Che la seconda morte ciascun grida:
E poi vedrai color, che son contenti
  Nel fuoco; perchè speran di venire,
  Quando che fia, alle beate genti:
Alle qua' poi se tu vorrai salire,
  Anima fia, a ciò di me più degna:
  Con lei ti lascerò nel mio partire:
Che quello 'mperador, che lassù regna,
  Perch' i' fu' ribellante alla sua legge,
  Non vuol che'n sua città per me si vegna.
In tutte parti impera, e quivi regge:
  Quivi è la sua cittade, e l'alto seggio:
  O felice colui, cu' ivi elegge!
Ed io a lui: Poeta, i' ti rechieggio,
  Per quello Iddio, che tu non conoscesti,
  Acciocch' i' fugga questo male e peggio,
Che tu mi meni, là dov'or dicesti,
  Sì ch' i' vegga la porta di san Pietro,
  E color che tu fai cotanto mesti.
Allor si mosse, ed io li tenni dietro.

CANTO II.

LO giorno se n'andava, e l'aer bruno
    Toglieva gli animai, che sono 'n terra,
Dalle fatiche loro: ed io sol' uno
                    M'apparecchiava

THIRD EPISTLE. 43

Where thou shalt see the tortur'd spirits roll,
   And hear each mourn his miserable fate,
   Calling for death on his immortal soul.
Then shalt thou visit those, who in a state
   Of purifying fire are still content,
   And for their promis'd heaven submissive wait:
If to that heaven thy happy course is bent,
   A worthier guard will soon my place supply;
   A purer spirit, for thy guidance sent!
For that Immortal Power, who rules on high,
   Because I ne'er his perfect laws have known,
   His sacred presence will to me deny.
There in the realms of light he fix'd his throne;
   There o'er the world Almighty Lord he reigns:
   O blest the servant whom he deigns to own!—
Poet (I answer'd) by thy living strains,
   And by that God, tho' not reveal'd to thee,
   That I may 'scape from these, and heavier pains,
Be thou my leader, where thy way is free!
   So that my eyes St. Peter's gate may find,
   And all the wonders of the deep may see!
He led, and I attentive march'd behind.

CANTO II.

THE day was sinking, and the dusky air
   On all the animals of earth bestow'd
   Rest from their labours. I alone prepare

M'apparecchiava a foſtener la guerra,
   Si del cammino, e sì della pietate,
   Che ritrarrà le mente, che non erra.
O Muſe, o alto 'ngegno, or m'ajutate:
   O mente, che ſcriveſti ciò ch'i' vidi,
   Qui ſi parrà la tua nobilitate.
Io cominciai: Poeta, che mi guidi,
   Guarda la mia virtù, s'ell' è poſſente,
   Prima ch' all' alto paſſo tu mi fidi.
Tu dici, che di Silvio lo parente,
   Corrutibile ancora, ad immortale
   Secolo andò, e fu ſenſibilmente.
Però ſe l'avverſario d'ogni male
   Corteſe fu, penſando l'alto effetto,
   Ch' uſcir dovea di lui, e 'l chi, e 'l quale,
Non pare indegno ad uomo d'intelletto:
   Ch' ei fu dell' alma Roma, e di ſuo 'mpero,
   Nell' empireo ciel, per padre, eletto:
La quale, e'l quale (a voler dir lo vero)
   Fur ſtabiliti, per lo loco ſanto,
   U' ſiede il ſucceſſor del maggior Piero.
Per queſta andata, onde li dai tu vanto,
   Inteſe coſe, che furon cagione
   Di ſua vittoria, e del papale ammanto.
Andovvi poi lo vas d'elezione,
   Per recarne conforto, a quella fede,
   Ch' è principio alla via di ſalvazione.

Ma

To meet new toil, both from my dreary road,
  And pious wish to paint in worthy phrase
  The Unerring Mind, and his divine abode.
O sacred Muses! now my genius raise!
  O Memory, who writest what I saw,
  From hence shall spring thy ever-during praise!
Kind Poet (I began, with trembling awe)
  Mark if my soul be equal to this aim!
  Nor into scenes too hard my weakness draw!
Thy Song declares, the Chief of pious fame
  Appear'd among the blest, retaining still
  His mortal senses and material frame;
Yet, if the great Opposer of all ill
  Shew'd grace to him, as knowing what and who
  Should from him rise, and mighty things fulfil,
Most worthy he appear'd, in Reason's view,
  That Heaven should chuse him as the Roman Sire,
  Scource of that empire which so widely grew,
Mark'd in its growth by the angelic choir
  To be the seat where Sanctity should rest,
  And Peter's heirs yet raise dominion higher.
From his dark journey, in thy Song exprest,
  He learn'd mysterious things; from whence arose
  Rome's early grandeur and the Papal vest.
To Paul, while living, heaven's high powers disclose
  Their secret bliss, that he may thence receive
  Strength in that faith from which salvation flows.

But

Ma io, perchè venirvi ? o chi 'l concede ?
  Io non Enea, io non Paolo fono:
  Me degno à ciò, nè io, nè altri il crede.
Perchè fe del venire i' m'abbandono,
  Temo che la venuta non fia folle :
  Se' favio, e 'ntendi me', ch'i' non ragiono.
E quale è quei, che difvuol ciò ch'e' volle,
  E per nuovi penfier cangia propofta,
  Si che del cominciar tutto fi tolle ;
Tal mi fec' io' in quella ofcura cofta :
  Perchè, penfando, confumai la 'mprefa,
  Che fu, nel cominciar, cotanto tofta.
Se io ho ben la tua parola intefa,
  Rifpofe del magnanimo quell' ombra,
  L'anima tua è da viltate offefa :
La qual molte fiate l'uomo ingombra,
  Si che d'onrata imprefa lo rivolve,
  Come falfo veder beftia, quand' ombra.
Da quefta tema acciocchè tu ti folve,
  Dirotti, perch' i' venni, e quel, ch'io'ntefi,
  Nel primo punto, che di te mi dolve.
Io era tra color, che fon fofpefi,
  E donna mi chiamò beata e bella,
  Tal che di comandare i' la richiefi.
Lucevan gli occhi fuoi più, che la ftella :
  E cominciommi a dir foave e piana,
  Con angelica voce, in fua favella :

THIRD EPISTLE.

But how may I this high exploit atchieve?
I'm not Æneas, nor the holy Paul:
Of this unworthy I myself believe:
If then I follow at thy friendly call,
   Midway perchance my trembling soul may sink:
   Wise as thou art, thou may'st foresee my fall.
Now as a man who, shudd'ring on the brink
   Of some great venture, sudden shifts his mind,
   And feels his spirit from the peril shrink;
So, in this scene of doubt and darkness join'd,
   Wavering I wasted thought in wild affright,
   And the first ardour of my soul resign'd.
If thy faint words I understand aright,
   (Reply'd the mighty and magnanimous shade)
   Those mists of fear have dimm'd thy mental sight,
Which oft the feat of human sense invade,-
   And make blind mortals from high deeds recoil,
   By Terror's airy phantasies betray'd:
But, that such fears thy soul no more may foil,
   I'll tell thee whence I came; at whose request;
   When first I pitied thy uncertain toil.
From the suspended host in which I rest,
   A lovely Spirit call'd me, fair as light;
   Eager I waited on her high behest;
While eyes beyond the solar radiance bright,
   And with the sweetness of an angel's tongue,
   Thus her soft words my willing aid invite:
                                  O ever

O'anima cortese Mantovana,
   Di cui la fama ancor nel mondo dura,
   E durerà, quanto 'l moto lontana:
L'amico mio, e non della ventura,
   Nella deserta piaggia è impedito
   Sì nel cammin, che volto è per paura:
E temo, che non sia già sì smarrito,
   Ch'io mi sia tardi al soccorso levata,
   Per quel, ch' io ho di lui, nel Cielo, udito.
Or muovi, e con la tua parola ornata,
   E con ciò, che ha mestieri al suo campare,
   L'ajuta sì, ch'i' ne sia consolata.
I' son Beatrice, che ti faccio andare:
   Vegno di loco, ove tornar disio:
   Amor mi mosse, che mi fa parlare.
Quando farò dinanzi al signor mio,
   Di te mi loderò sovente a lui:
   Tacette allora, e poi comincia' io:
O donna di virtù, sola, per cui,
   L'umana spezie eccede ogni contento
   Da quel ciel, ch' ha minor li cerchi suoi:
Tanto m'aggrada 'l tuo comandamento,
   Che l'ubbidir, se già fosse, m'è tardi:
   Più non t'è uopo aprirmi 'l tuo talento.
Ma dimmi la cagion, che non ti guardi
   Dello scender quaggiuso, in questo centro,
   Dall' ampio loco, ove tornar tu ardi.

THIRD EPISTLE.

O ever gentle shade, from Mantua sprung!
   Whose fame unfading on the earth shall last
   As long as earth in ambient air is hung;
My friend, whose love all base desire surpast,
   In yon drear desart finds his passage barr'd,
   And compass'd round with terrors stands aghast;
And much I fear, beset with dangers hard,
   He may be lost beyond all friendly reach,
   And I from heaven descend too late a guard.
But go! and with thy soft soul-soothing speech,
   And all the aid thy wisdom may inspire,
   The ways of safety to this wanderer teach!
My name is Beatrice: the heavenly quire
   For this I left, tho' ever left with pain;
   But love suggested what I now desire.
When I the presence of my lord regain,
   On thee my praises with delight shall dwell.
   So spake this angel, in her heavenly strain.
Bright Fair, (I cry'd) who didst on earth excel
   All that e'er shone beneath the lunar sphere,
   And every mind to virtuous love impel!
Had I e'en now perform'd the task I hear,
   That swift performance I should think too slow:
   Nor needs there more; your gracious will is clear:
Yet how you venture, I would gladly know,
   From those pure realms, to which again you fly,
   So near the center of eternal woe.

Da che tu vuoi saper cotanto addentro,
  Dirotti brevemente, mi rispose,
  Perch' i' non temo di venir qua entro.
Temer si dee di sole quelle cose,
  Ch' hanno potenza di fare altrui male :
  Dell' altre nò, che non son paurose.
Io son fatta da Dio, sua mercè, tale,
  Che la vostra miseria non mi tange,
  Nè fiamma d'esto 'hcendio non m'assale.
Donna è gentil nel ciel, che si compiange
  Di questo 'mpedimento, ov' i' ti mando,
  Sì che duro giudicio lassù frange.
Questa chiese Lucìa in suo dimando,
  E disse : Ora abbisogna il tuo fedele
  Di te, ed io a te lo raccomando.
Lucìa nimica di ciascun crudele
  Si mosse, e venne al loco, dov' i' era,
  Che mi sedea con l'antica Rachele :
Disse, Beatrice, loda di Dio vera,
  Che non soccorri quei, che t'amò tanto;
  Ch' uscìo per te della volgare schiera ?
Non odi tu la pieta del suo pianto,
  Non vedi tu la morte, che 'l combatte
  Su la fiumana, ove 'l mar non ha vanto ?
Al mondo non fur mai persone ratte
  A far lor pro, ed a fuggir lor danno,
  Com' io, dopo cotai parole satte,

                              Venni

THIRD EPISTLE.

What you require (she said, in kind reply)
   I briefly will explain: how thus I dare,
   Unconscious of alarm, these depths to try.
From these things only springs our fearful care,
   By which our hapless friends may suffer ill;
   But not from other; for no fear is there.
Such am I form'd, by Heaven's most gracious will,
   That torture cannot touch my purer frame,
   E'en where fierce fires his flaming region fill.
A gentle spirit (Lucia is her name)
   In heaven laments the hardships of my friend,
   For whom I ask your aid: to me she came,
And kindly bade me to his woes attend:
   Behold (she said) thy servant in distress!
   And I his safety to thy care commend.
Lucia, the friend of all whom ills oppress,
   Me, where I sate with pensive Rachel, sought,
   In heavenly contemplation's deep recess:
In mercy's name (she cry'd) thus lost in thought,
   Seest thou not him who held thy charms so dear,
   Whom Love to rise above the vulgar taught?
And dost thou not his lamentation hear,
   Nor see the horror, which his strength impairs,
   On yon wide torrent, with no haven near?
Never was mind, intent on worldly cares,
   So eager wealth to gain, or loss to shun,
   As, when acquainted with these deadly snares,

Venni quaggiù dal mio beato scanno,
  Fidandomi nel tuo parlare onesto,
  Ch' onora te, e quei, ch'udito l'hanno.
Poscia che m'ebbe ragionato questo,
  Gli occhi lucenti, lagrimando, volse:
  Perchè mi fece del venir più presto:
E venni à te così, com' ella volse:
  Dinanzi a quella fiera ti levai,
  Che del bel monte il corto andar ti tolse,
Dunque che è? perchè, perchè ristai?
  Perchè tanta viltà nel cuore allette?
  Perchè ardire e franchezza non hai?
Poscia che tai tre donne benedette
  Curan di te, nella corte del Cielo,
  E'l mio parlar tanto ben t'impromette?
Quale i fioretti, dal notturno gielo,
  Chinati e chiusi, poi che'l sol gl'imbianca,
  Si drizzan tutti aperti in loro stelo,
Tal mi fec' io, di mia virtute stanca:
  E tanto buono ardire al cuor mi corse,
  Ch' i' cominciai, come persona franca:
O pietosa colei, che mi soccorse,
  E tu cortese, ch' ubbidisti tosto
  Alle vere parole, che ti porse!
Tu m'hai con desiderio il cuor disposto
  Sì al venir, con le parole tue,
  Ch'i' son tornato nel primo proposto,

Or

THIRD EPISTLE.

I flew from the bleft confines of the fun,
  Trufting that eloquence, which to thy name
  And to thy followers fuch praife has won.
She having thus explain'd her gracious aim,
  Turn'd her bright eyes, which tears of pity fill:
  And hence more fwift to thy relief I came;
And, pleas'd to execute her heavenly will,
  I fav'd thee from the fury of that Beaft,
  Which barr'd thy journey up the brighter hill.
Why then, O why has all thy ardour ceas'd?
  And whence this faintnefs in thy feeble mind?
  Why has its noble energy decreas'd,
When thefe pure Spirits, for thy good combin'd,
  Watch o'er thy fafety in their heavenly feat,
  And I reveal the favour thou fhalt find?—
As tender flowers, reviv'd by folar heat,
  That thro' the chilling night have funk depreft,
  Rife and unfold, the welcome ray to meet;
So rofe my fpirit, of new life poffeft;
  And, my warm heart on high atchievements bent,
  I thus my animating guide addreft:
Gracious that Spirit who thy fuccour fent!
  And friendly thou, who freely haft difplay'd
  Thy zeal to execute her kind intent!
Thy foothing words have to my foul convey'd
  Such keen defire to thofe bright realms to foar,
  I fcorn the terror that my ftep delay'd.

Or va, ch'un fol volere è d'amendue:
  Tu duca, tu fignore, e tu maeftro:
  Così li diffi: e poichè moffo fue,
Entrai per lo cammino alto e filveftro.

CANTO III.

" PER me fi va nella città dolente:
    Per me fi va nell' eterno dolore:
  Per me fi va tra la perduta gente.
Giuftizia moffe 'l mio alto fattore:
  Fecemi la divina poteftate,
  La fomma fapienzia, e 'l primo amore.
Dinanzi a me non fur cofe create,
  Se non eterne, ed io eterno duro:
  Lafciate ogni fperanza, voi che 'ntrate."—
Quefte parole di colore ofcuro
  Vid' io fcritte al fommo d'una porta:
  Perch'io, Maeftro, il fenfo lor m'è duro.
Ed egli a me, come perfona accorta,
  Qui fi convien lafciare ogni fofpetto:
  Ogni viltà convien, che qui fia morta.
Noi fem venuti al luogo, ov' i' t'ho detto,
  Che tu vedrai le genti dolorofe,
  Ch' hanno perduto 'l ben dello 'ntelletto.
                                E poichè

Now lead!—thy pleasure I dispute no more.
   My lord, my master thou! and thou my guard!—
   I ended here; and, while he march'd before,
The gloomy road I enter'd, deep and hard.

CANTO III.

"THRO' me you pass to Mourning's dark domain;
   Thro' me, to scenes where Grief must ever pine;
   Thro' me, to Misery's devoted train.
Justice and power in my Great Founder join,
   And love and wisdom all his fabrics rear;
   Wisdom above controul, and love divine!
Before me, Nature saw no works appear.
   Save works eternal: such was I ordain'd.
   Quit every hope, all ye who enter here!"—
These characters, where misty darkness reign'd,
   High o'er a lofty gate I saw engrav'd.
   Ah Sire! (said I) hard things are here contain'd.
He, sapient Guide! my farther question sav'd,
   With spirit answering, "Here all doubt resign,
   All weak distrust, and every thought deprav'd;
At length we've reach'd that gloomy drear confine,
   Where, as I said, thou'lt see the mournful race
   For ever robb'd of Reason's light benign."
                            Then,

E poichè la fua mano alla mia pofe,
   Con lieto volto, ond' i' mi confortai,
   Mi mife dentro alle fegrete cofe.
Quivi fofpiri, pianti, e alti guai
   Rifonavan, per l'aer fenza ftelle,
   Perch'io al cominciar, ne lagrimai.
Diverfe lingue, orribili favelle,
   Parole di dolore, accenti d'ira,
   Voci alte e fioche, e fuon di man con elle
Facevano un tumulto, il qual s'aggira
   Sempre 'n quell' aria, fenza tempo, tinta,
   Come la rena quando 'l turbo fpira.
Ed io, ch' avea d' error la tefta cinta,
   Diffi, Maeftro, che è quel, ch' i' odo?
   E che gent' è, che par nel duol sì vinta?
Ed egli a me: Quefto mifero modo
   Tengon l' anime trifte di coloro,
   Che viffer fanza infamia, e fanza lodo.
Mifchiate fono a quel cattivo coro
   Degli angeli, che non furon ribelli,
   Nè fur fedeli a Dio, ma per fe foro.
Cacciarli i ciel, per non effer men belli;
   Nè lo profondo inferno gli riceve,
   Ch' alcuna gloria i rei avrebber d'elli.
Ed io: Maeftro, che è tanto greve
   A lor, che lamentar gli fa sì forte?
   Rifpofe: Dicerolti molto breve.

                          Questi

THIRD EPISTLE.

Then, stretching forth his hand with gentle grace,
   From whence new comfort thro' my bosom flows,
   He led me in to that mysterious place.
There sighs, and wailings, and severest woes,
   Deeply resounded through the starless air;
   And as I first advanc'd, my fears arose.
Each different cry, the murmuring notes of care,
   Accents of misery, and words of ire,
   With all the sounds of discord and despair,
To form such tumult in this scene conspire,
   As flies for ever round the gloomy waste,
   Like sand when quicken'd by the whirlwind's fire.
I then (my mind with error still disgrac'd)
   Exclaim'd—O Sire! what may this trouble mean?
   What forms are these by sorrow so debas'd?—
He soon reply'd—Behold, these bounds between,
   All who without or infamy or fame
   Clos'd the blank business of their mortal scene!
They join those angels, of ignoble name,
   Who not rebell'd, yet were not faithful found;
   Without attachment! self alone their aim!
Heaven shuts them out from its unsullied bound:
   And Hell refuses to admit this train,
   Lest e'en the damn'd o'er these their triumphs found.
O Sire! (said I) whence then this grievous pain,
   That on our ears their lamentations grate?—
   This (he reply'd, I will in brief explain:

                         These

Questi non hanno speranza di morte:
 E la lor cieca vita è tanto bassa,
 Che 'nvidiosi son d'ogni altra sorte.
Fama di loro il mondo esser non lassa:
 Misericordia e giustizia gli sdegna.
 Non ragioniam di lor, ma guarda, e passa.
Ed io, che riguardai, vidi una insegna,
 Che, girando, correva tanto ratta,
 Che d'ogni posa mi pareva indegna:
E dietro le venía sì lunga tratta
 Di gente, ch'i' non avrei mai creduto,
 Che morte tanta n' avesse disfatta.
Poscia ch' io v'ebbi alcun riconosciuto,
 Guardai, e vidi l'ombra di colui,
 Che fece, per viltate, il gran rifiuto.
Incontanente intese, e certo fui,
 Che quest' era la setta de' cattivi
 A Dio spiacenti, ed a' nemici sui.
Questi sciaurati, che mai non fur vivi,
 Erano ignudi, e stimolati molto
 Da mosconi, e da vespe, ch'erano ivi.
Elle rigavan lor di sangue il volto,
 Che mischiato di lagrime, a' lor piedi,
 Da fastidiosi vermi era ricolto.
E poi, ch'a riguardare oltre mi diedi,
 Vidi gente alla riva d'un gran fiume;
 Perch' i' dissi: Maestro, or mi concedi,

Ch'io

These have no hope that death may mend their fate;
  And their blind days form so confus'd a mass,
  They pine with envy of each other's state:
From earth their name has perish'd like the grass;
  E'en Mercy views them with a scornful eye.
  We'll speak of them no more: Behold! and pass!—
I look'd, and saw a banner rais'd on high,
  That whirl'd, unconscious of a moment's stand,
  With rapid circles in the troubled sky:
Behind it, driven by Fate's supreme command,
  Came such a host! I ne'er could have believ'd
  Death had collected so complete a band.
When now I had the forms of all perceiv'd,
  I saw the shade of that ignoble priest,
  Of sovereign power by indolence bereav'd.
Instant I knew, from every doubt releas'd,
  These were the base, the miscreated crew
  To whom the hate of God had never ceas'd.
Vile forms! ne'er honor'd with existence true!
  Naked they march'd, and sorely were they stung
  By wasps and hornets, that around them flew;
These the black blood from their gall'd faces wrung;
  Blood mixt with tears, that, trickling to their feet,
  Fed the fastidious worms which round them clung.
When now I farther pierc'd the dark retreat,
  Numbers I saw beside a mighty stream:
  Sudden I cry'd—Now, Sire, let me entreat
      To

Ch' io fappia, quali fono, e qual coſtume
　Le fa parer di trapaſſar sì pronte,
　Com' io diſcerno per lo fioco lume.
Ed egli a me: Le coſe ti fien conte,
　Quando noi fermerem li noſtri paſſi
　Su la triſta riviera d'Acheronte.
Allor con gli occhi vergognoſi e baſſi
　Temendo, no 'l mio dir gli fuſſe grave,
　Infino al fiume di parlar mi traſſi.
Ed ecco verſo noi venir, per nave,
　Un vecchio bianco, per antico pelo,
　Gridando, Guai à voi anime prave:
Non iſperate mai veder lo cielo:
　I' vegno, per menarvi all' altra riva
　Nelle tenebre eterne, in caldo e'n gielo
E tu, che fe' coſtì, anima viva,
　Partiti da coteſti, che ſon morti :
　Ma poi ch' e' vide, ch' i' non mi partiva,
Diſſe: Per altre vie, per altri porti
　Verrai a piaggia, non qui, per paſſare:
　Più lieve legno convien, che ti porti.
E'l duca à lui: Caron, non ti crucciare:
　Vuolſi così colà, dove ſi puote
　Ciò che ſi vuole, e più non dimandare.
Quinci fur quete le lanoſe gote
　Al nocchier della livida palude,
　Che 'ntorno agli occhi ave' di fiamme ruote.

　　　　　　　　　　　　　　　　Ma

THIRD EPISTLE.

To know what forms in diftant profpect feem
   To pafs fo fwiftly o'er a flood fo wide,
   As I difcern by this imperfect gleam?—
That fhalt thou know (return'd my gracious Guide)
   When the near refpite from our toil we reach,
   On fullen Acheron's infernal tide.—
With downcaft eyes, that pardon now befeech,
   And hoping filence may that pardon win,
   E'en to the river I abftain'd from fpeech.
And lo! towards us, with a fhrivell'd fkin,
   A hoary boatman fteers his crazy bark,
   Exclaiming, "Woe to all ye fons of fin!
Hope not for heaven, nor light's celeftial fpark!
   I come to waft you to a different lot;
   To Torture's realm, with endlefs horror dark:
And thou, who living view'ft this facred fpot,
   Hafte to depart from thefe, for thefe are dead!"
   But when he faw that I departed not,
In wrath he cry'd, "Thro' other paffes led,
   Not here, fhalt thou attempt the farther fhore;
   But in a bark to bear thy firmer tread."—
O Charon, faid my Guide, thy ftrife give o'er;
   For thus 'tis will'd in that fuperior fcene
   Where will is power. Seek thou to know no more!—
Now grew the bearded vifage more ferene
   Of the ftern boatman on the livid lake,
   Whofe eyes fo lately glar'd with anger keen:

                                      But

Ma quell' anime, ch' eran laſſe e nude,
   Cangiar colore, e dibattero i denti,
   Ratto che 'nteſer le parole crude.
Beſtemmiavano Iddio, e i lor parenti,
   L'umana ſpezie, il luogo, il tempo, e'l ſeme,
   Di lor ſemenza, e di lor naſcimenti.
Poi ſi ritraſſer tutte quante inſieme.
   Forte piangendo, alla riva malvagia,
   Ch'attende ciaſcun' uom, che Dio non teme.
Caron dimonio, con occhi di bragia,
   Loro accennando, tutte le raccoglie:
   Batte col remo, qualunque s' adagia.
Come d' Autunno ſi levan le foglie,
   L' una appreſſo dell' altra, infin che 'l ramo
   Rende alla terra tutte le ſue ſpoglie;
Similemente il mal ſeme d'Adamo:
   Gittanſi di quel lito ad una ad una,
   Per cenni, com' augel, per ſuo richiamo.
Così ſen vanno ſu per l'onda bruna,
   E avanti che ſien di là diſceſe,
   Anche di qua nova ſchiera s'aduna.
Figliuol mio, diſſe il maeſtro corteſe,
   Quelli, che muojon nell' ira di Dio,
   Tutti convegnon qui d' ogni paeſe:
E pronti ſono al trapaſſar del rio,
   Che la divina giuſtizia gli ſprona,
   Sì che la tema ſi volge in diſio.

                                          Quinci

THIRD EPISTLE.

But all the naked shades began to quake;
   Their shuddering figures grew more pale than earth,
   Soon as they heard the cruel words he spake:
God they blasphem'd, their parents' injur'd worth,
   And all mankind; the place, the hour, that saw
   Their first formation, and their future birth.
Then were they driven, by Fate's resistless law,
   Weeping, to that sad scene prepar'd for all
   Who fear not God with pure devotion's awe.
Charon, with eyes of fire and words of gall,
   Collects his crew, and high his oar he wields,
   To strike the tardy wretch who slights his call.
As leaves in autumn thro' the woody fields
   Fly in succession, when each trembling tree
   Its ling'ring honors to the whirlwind yields;
So this bad race, condemn'd by Heaven's decree,
   Successive hasten from that river's side:
   As birds, which at a call to bondage flee,
So are they wafted o'er the gloomy tide;
   And ere from thence their journey is begun,
   A second crew awaits their hoary guide.—
My gracious Master kindly said —My son!
   All those who in the wrath of God expire,
   From every clime haste hither, one by one;
Nor would their terrors from this stream retire,
   Since heavenly justice so impels their mind,
   That fear is quicken'd into keen desire.
                                Here

Quinci non paffa mai anima buona:
 E però fe Caron di te fi lagna,
 Ben puoi faper omai, che'l fuo dir fuona.
Finito quefto la buja campagna
 Tremò sì forte, che dello fpavento
 La mente di fudore ancor mi bagna.
La terra lagrimofa diede vento,
 Che balenò una luce vermiglia,
 La qual mi vinfe ciafcun fentimento:
E caddi, come l' uom, cui fonno piglia.

NOTE V. VERSE 127.

The gay Boccacio tempts th' Italian Muse.] Boccacio was almoft utterly unknown to our country as a Poet, when two of our moft accomplifhed Critics reftored his poetical reputation.

Mr. Tyrwhitt, to whom Chaucer is as deeply indebted as a Poet can be to the judgment and erudition of his commentator, has given a fketch of Boccacio's Thefeida, in his introductory difcourfe to the Canterbury Tales; and Mr. Warton has enriched the firft volume of his Hiftory of Englifh Poetry with a confiderable fpecimen of this very rare Italian Epic poem, of which our country is faid to poffefs but a fingle copy.—The father of Boccacio was an Italian merchant, a native

THIRD EPISTLE.

Here may no spirit pass, to good inclin'd;
   And hence, if Charon seem'd to thwart thy will,
   Hence wilt thou deem his purpose not unkind.—
He paus'd; and horrors of approaching ill
   Now made the mournful troop so stand aghast,
   Their fears yet strike me with a deadly chill!
The groaning earth sent forth a hollow blast,
   And flash'd a fiery glare of gloomy red!
   The horrid scene my fainting power surpast:
I fell, and, as in sleep, my senses fled.

---

tive of Certaldo, near Florence, who in his travels attached himself to a young woman of Paris; and our Poet is supposed to have been the illegitimate offspring of that connection. He was born in 1313, and educated as a student of the canon law; but a sight of Virgil's tomb, according to Filippo Villani, his most ancient Biographer, made him resolve to relinquish his more irksome pursuits, and devote himself entirely to the Muses. His life seems to have been divided between literature and love, as he was equally remarkable for an amorous disposition, and a passionate attachment to study. His most celebrated mistress was Mary of Arragon, the natural daughter of Robert, King of Naples, the generous and enthusiastic patron of Petrarch. To this lady, distinguished by the name of The Fiammetta, Boccacio addreffed his capital poem, the Thefeida; telling her, in an introductory letter, that it contained many allufions to the particular circumftances of their own fecret attachment. In his latter days he retired to Certaldo, and died there in the year 1475, of a diforder fuppofed to have arifen from exceffive application. Few authors have rendered more effential fervice to the republic of letters than Boccacio, as he not only contributed very much to the improvement of his native language, but was particularly inftrumental in promoting the revival of ancient learning: a merit which he fhared with Petrarch. The tender and generous friendfhip which fubfifted between thefe two engaging authors, reflects the higheft honour on both; and their letters to each other may be ranked among the moft interefting productions of that period. Boccacio compofed, according to Quadrio, no lefs than thirty-four volumes. His Novels are univerfally known: his Poetical Works are as follow: 1. La Thefeida, in Ottava Rima. 2. L'Amorofa Vifione, in Terza Rima. 3. Il Filoftrato, in Ottava Rima. 4. Il Ninfale Fiefolano, in Ottava Rima.—He piqued himfelf on being the firft Poet who fung of martial fubjects in Italian verfe; and he has been generally fuppofed the inventor of the Ottava Rima, the common Heroic meafure of the Italian Mufe: but Quadrio has fhewn that it was ufed by preceding writers; and Pafquier, in his Recherches, has quoted two ftanzas of Thibaud King of Navarre, written in the fame meafure, on Blanch queen of France, who died in 1252. The neglect into which the Poems of Boccacio had fallen appears the more ftriking, as he peculiarly prided himfelf on his poetical character; informing the world, by an infcription on his tomb, that Poetry was his favourite purfuit—Studium fuit alma Poefis, are the laft words of the epitaph which he compofed for himfelf.

NOTE VI. VERSE 142.

She fpoke exulting, and Triffino fung.] Giovanni Giorgio Triffino was born of a noble family in Vicenza, 1478: he was particularly diftinguifhed by a paffion for Poetry and Architecture; and one of the very few Poets who have been rich enough to build a palace. This he is faid to have done from a defign of his own, under the direction of the celebrated Palladio. He had the merit of writing the firft regular tragedy in the Italian language, entitled Sophonifba; but in his Epic poem he is generally allowed to have failed, though fome learned Critics (and Gravina amongft them) have
endeavoured

endeavoured to support the credit of that performance. His subject was the expulsion of the Goths from Italy by Belisarius; and his poem consists of twenty-seven books, in blank verse. He addressed it to the Emperor Charles the Vth; and professes in his Dedication to have taken Aristotle for his preceptor, and Homer for his guide.

The reader will excuse a trifling anachronism, in my naming Trissino before Ariosto, for poetical reasons. The Italia Liberata of the former was first published in 1548; the Orlando Furioso, in 1515. Trissino died at Rome, 1550; Ariosto at Ferrara, 1533.

NOTE VII. VERSE 194.

Of a poetic Sire the more poetic Son.] The reputation of Torquato Tasso has almost eclipsed that of his father Bernardo, who was himself a considerable Poet, and left two productions of the Epic kind, L'Amadigi, and Il Floridante: the latter remained unfinished at his death, but was afterwards published in its imperfect state by his son; who has spoken of his father's poetry with filial regard, in his different critical works. The Amadigi

THIRD EPISTLE. 69

digi was written at the requeſt of ſeveral Spaniſh Grandees, in the court of Charles the Vth, and firſt printed in Venice by Giolito, 1560. The curious reader may find an entertaining account of the Author's ideas in compoſing this work, among his Letters, volume the firſt, page 198. I cannot help remarking, that the letter referred to contains a ſimile which Torquato has introduced in the opening of his Jeruſalem Delivered.

The Italians have formed a very pleaſing and valuable work, by collecting the letters of their eminent Painters; which contain much information on points relating to their art. The letters of their Poets, if properly ſelected, might alſo form a few intereſting volumes: as a proof of this, I ſhall inſert a ſhort letter of the younger Taſſo, becauſe it ſeems to have eſcaped the notice of his Biographers, and relates the remarkable circumſtance of his having deliberated on five different ſubjects before he decided in favour of Goffredo:

Al M. Illuſtre Sig. Conte Ferrante Eſtenſe Taſſone,

Io ho ſcritto queſta mattina a V. S. che io deſidero di far due Poemi a mio guſto; e ſebben per elezione non cambierei il ſoggetto che una volta preſi; nondimeno per ſoddisfar il ſignor principe gli do l'elezione di tutti questi soggetti, i quali mi paiono sovra gli altri atti a ricever la forma eroica.

Espedizion di Goffredo, e degli altri principi contra gl' Infedeli, e ritorno. Dove avrò occasione di lodar le famiglie d' Europa, che io vorrò.

Espedizion di Belisario contra i Goti.

Di Narsete contra i Goti, e discorro d' un principe. E in questi avrei grandissima occasione di lodar le cose di Spagna e d' Italia e di Grecia e l' origine di casa d' Austria.

Espedizion di Carlo il magno contra Lansoni.

Espedizion di Carlo contra i Longobardi. In questi troverei l' origine di tutte le famiglie grandi di Germania, di Francia, e d' Italia, e 'l ritorno d' un principe.

E sebben alcuni di questi soggetti sono stati presi, non importa; perche io cercherei di trattargli meglio, e a giudicio d' Aristotele.

Opere di Torquato Tasso, tom. ix. p. 240.

This letter is the more worthy of notice, as the subject on which Tasso fixed has been called by Voltaire, and perhaps very justly, Le plus grand qu'on ait jamais choisi. Le Tasse l'a traité dignement, adds the lively Critic, with unusual candour;

THIRD EPISTLE. 71

dour; yet in his subsequent remarks he is peculiarly severe on the magic of the Italian Poet. The merits of Tasso are very ably defended against the injustice of French criticism, and particularly that of Boileau and Voltaire, in the well-known Letters on Chivalry and Romance. Indeed the genius of this injured Poet seems at length to triumph in the country where he was most insulted, as the French have lately attempted a poetical version of his Jerusalem.

I enter not into the history of Tasso, or that of his rival Ariosto, because the public has lately received from Mr. Hoole a judicious account of their lives, prefixed to his elegant versions of their respective Poems.

NOTE VIII. VERSE 197.

Shall gay Tassoni want his festive crown.] Alessandro Tassoni, the supposed inventor of the modern Heroi-comic Poetry, was born at Modena, 1565. His family was noble; but his parents dying during his infancy, left him exposed to vexatious law-suits, which absorbed a great part of his patrimony, and rendered him dependant. In 1599 he was engaged as Secretary to Cardinal Ascanio Colonna,

Colonna, whom he attended on an embassy into Spain. He was occasionally dispatched into Italy on the service of that Prelate, and in the course of one of these expeditions wrote his Observations on Petrarch. In 1605 he is supposed to have quitted the service of the Cardinal, and to have lived in a state of freedom at Rome, where, in 1607, he became the chief of a literary society, intitled Academia degli Umoristi. He was afterwards employed in the service of Charles Emanuel, Duke of Savoy; which, after suffering many vexations in it, he quitted with a design of devoting himself to study and retirement. But this design he was induced to relinquish, and to serve the Cardinal Lodovisio, nephew of Pope Gregory XV. from whom he received a considerable stipend. On the death of this patron, in 1632, he was recalled to his native city by Francis the First, Duke of Modena, and obtained an honourable establishment in the court of that Prince. Age had now rendered him unable to enjoy his good fortune: his health declined in the year of his return, and he expired in April 1635. His genius was particularly disposed to lively satire; and the incidents of his life had a tendency to increase that disposition. After having passed many vexatious and unprofitable years in

the

the service of the Great, he had his portrait painted, with a fig in his hand; and Muratori supposes him to have written these two lines on the occasion:

Dextera cur ficum, quæris, mea gestet inanem:
Longi operis merces hæc fuit; aula dedit.

His celebrated Poem, La Secchia rapita, was written, as he has himself declared, in 1611; begun in April, and finished in October. It was circulated in MS. received wth the utmost avidity, and first printed at Paris 1622. In a catalogue of the numerous editions of the Secchia, which Muratori has prefixed to his Life of Tassoni, he includes an English translation of it, printed 1715.

NOTE IX. VERSE 209.

And rashly judges that her Vega's lyre.] The famous Lope de Vega, frequently called the Shakespear of Spain, is perhaps the most fertile Poet in the annals of Parnassus; and it would be difficult to name any author, ancient or modern, so universally idolized while living by all ranks of people, and so magnificently rewarded by the liberality of the Great. He was the son of Felix de Vega and Francisca Fernandez, who were both descended from honourable

able families, and lived in the neighbourhood of Madrid. Our Poet was born in that city, on the 25th of November 1562. He was, according to his own expreſſion, a Poet from his cradle; and, beginning to make verſes before he had learned to write, he uſed to bribe his elder ſchool-fellows with a part of his breakfaſt, to commit to paper the lines he had compoſed. Having loſt his father while he was ſtill a child, he engaged in a frolic, very natural to a lively boy, and wandered with another lad to various parts of Spain, till, having ſpent their money, and being conducted before a magiſtrate at Segovia, for offering to ſell a few trinkets, they were ſent home again to Madrid. Soon after this adventure, our young Poet was taken under the protection of Geronimo Manrique, Biſhop of Avila, and began to diſtinguiſh himſelf by his dramatic compoſitions, which were received with great applauſe by the public, though their author had not yet completed his education; for, after this period, he became a member of the univerſity of Alcala, where he devoted himſelf for four years to the ſtudy of philoſophy. He was then engaged as Secretary to the Duke of Alva, and wrote his Arcadia in compliment to that patron; who is frequently mentioned in his Occaſional Poems. He quitted that employment on his marriage with Iſabel de
Urbina,

Urbina, a lady (fays his friend and biographer Perez de Montalvan) beautiful without artifice, and virtuous without affectation. His domestic happiness was soon interrupted by a painful incident:—Having written some lively verses in ridicule of a person who had taken some injurious freedom with his character, he received a challenge in consequence of his wit; and happening, in the duel which ensued, to give his adversary a dangerous wound, he was obliged to fly from his family, and shelter himself in Valencia. He resided there a considerable time; but connubial affection recalled him to Madrid. His wife died in the year of his return. His affliction on this event led him to relinquish his favourite studies, and embark on board the Armada which was then preparing for the invasion of England. He had a brother who served in that fleet as a lieutenant; and being shot in an engagement with some Dutch vessels, his virtues were celebrated by our afflicted Poet, whose heart was peculiarly alive to every generous affection. After the ill success of the Armada, the disconsolate Lope de Vega returned to Madrid, and became Secretary to the Marquis of Malpica, to whom he has addressed a grateful Sonnet. From the service of this Patron he passed into the household of the Count of Lemos, whom he celebrates as an ini-

mitable

mitable Poet. He was once more induced to quit his attendance on the Great, for the more inviting comforts of a married life. His second choice was Juana de Guardio, of noble birth and singular beauty. By this lady he had two children; a son, who died in his infancy, and a daughter, named Feliciana, who survived her father. The death of his little boy is said to have hastened that of his wife, whom he had the misfortune to lose in about seven years after his marriage. Having now experienced the precariousness of all human enjoyments, he devoted himself to a religious life, and fulfilled all the duties of it with the most exemplary piety; still continuing to produce an astonishing variety of poetical compositions. His talents and his virtues procured him many unsolicited honours. Pope Urban the VIIIth sent him the Cross of Malta, with the title of Doctor in Divinity, and appointed him to a place of profit in the Apostolic Chamber; favours for which he expressed his gratitude by dedicating his Corona Tragica (a long poem on the fate of Mary Queen of Scots) to that liberal Pontiff. In his seventy-third year he felt the approaches of death, and prepared himself for it with the utmost composure and devotion. His last hours were attended by many of his intimate friends, and particularly his chief patron the Duke of Sessa, whom

he

THIRD EPISTLE. 77

he made his executor; leaving him the care of his daughter Feliciana, and of his various manuscripts. The manner in which he took leave of those he loved was most tender and affecting. He said to his Disciple and Biographer, Montalvan, That true fame consisted in being good; and that he would willingly exchange all the applauses he had received, to add a single deed of virtue to the actions of his life. Having given his dying benediction to his daughter, and performed the last ceremonies of his religion, he expired on the 25th of August 1635.

The splendor of his funeral was equal to the respect paid to him while living.—His magnificent patron, the Duke of Sessa, invited the chief nobility of the kingdom to attend it. The ceremony was prolonged through the course of several days; and three sermons in honour of the deceased were delivered by three of the most celebrated preachers. These are printed with the works of the Poet, and may be considered as curious specimens of the false eloquence which prevailed at that time. A volume of encomiastic verses, chiefly Spanish, and written by more than a hundred and fifty of the most distinguished characters in Spain, was published soon after the death of this lamented Bard. To this collection his friend and disciple Perez de
                                                Montalvan

Montalvan prefixed a circumftantial account of his life and death, which I have chiefly followed in the preceding narrative. An ingenious Traveller, who has lately publifhed a pleafing volume of Letters on the Poetry of Spain, has imputed the duel, in which Lope de Vega was engaged, to the gallantries of his firft wife; but Montalvan's relation of that adventure clears the honour of the lady, whofe innocence is ftill farther fupported by a poem written in her praife by Pedro de Medina Medinilla: it is printed in the works of our Poet, who is introduced in it, under the name of Belardo, celebrating the excellencies and lamenting the lofs of his departed Ifabel.

Of the perfon and manners of Lope de Vega, his friend Montalvan has only given this general account:—that his frame of body was particularly ftrong, and preferved by temperance in continued health;—that in converfation he was mild and unaffuming; courteous to all, and to women peculiarly gallant;—very eager when engaged in the bufinefs of his friends, and fomewhat carelefs in the management of his own. Of his wealth and charity I fhall have occafion to fpeak in a fubfequent note. The chief expences in which he indulged himfelf were books and pictures; of the latter, he diftributed a few as legacies to his intimate friends:

to the Duke of Sessa, a fine portrait of himself; and to me, says Montalvan, another, painted when he was young, surrounded by dogs, monkies, and other monsters, and writing in the midst of them, without attending to their noise.——Of the honours paid to this extraordinary Poet, his Biographer asserts that no person of eminence visited Spain without seeking his personal acquaintance; that men yielded him precedence when they met him in the streets, and women saluted him with benedictions when he passed under their windows. If such homage can be deserved by the most unwearied application to poetry, Lope de Vega was certainly entitled to it. He declared that he constantly wrote five sheets a day; and his biographers, who have formed a calculation from this account, conclude the number of his verses to be no less than 21,316,000. His country has very lately published an elegant edition of his poems in 19 quarto volumes; his dramatic works are to be added to this collection, and will probably be still more voluminous. I shall speak only of the former.—Among his poems there are several of the Epic kind; the three following appear to me the most remarkable. 1. La Dragontea. 2. La Hermosura de Angelica. 3. La Jerusalem Conquistada. The Dragontea consists of ten cantos, on the last expedition and death of our great naval hero Sir Francis Drake; whom the Poet, from his exceffive partiality to his country, confiders as an avaricious pirate, or rather, as he chufes to call him, a marine Dragon: and it may be fufficient to obferve that he has treated him accordingly. The poem on Angelica feems to have been written in emulation of Ariofto, and it is founded on a hint in that Poet: it was compofed in the early part of our Author's life, and contains many compliments to his fovereign Philip the IId: it confifts of 20 cantos, and clofes with Angelica's being reftored to her beloved Medoro. In his Jerufalem Conquiftada he enters the lifts with Taffo, whom he mentions in his preface as having fung the firft part of the hiftory which he had chofen for his fubject. From the great name of Lope de Vega, I had fome thoughts of prefenting to the reader a fketch of this his moft remarkable poem; but as an Epic Poet he appears to me fo much inferior to Taffo, and to his countryman and cotemporary Ercilla, that I am unwilling to fwell thefe extenfive notes by an enlarged defcription of fo unfuccefsful a work: the Author has prophefied, in the clofe of it, that, although neglected by his own age, it would be efteemed by futurity:—a fingular proof that even the moft favoured writers are frequently difpofed to declaim againft the period in which they live.

THIRD EPISTLE.

live. If Lope de Vega could think himself neglected, what Poet may ever expect to be satisfied with popular applause?—But to return to his Jerusalem Conquistada. Richard the Second of England, and Alphonso the Eighth of Castile, are the chief heroes of the poem; which contains twenty cantos, and closes with the unfortunate return of these confederate Kings, and the death of Saladin. It was first printed 1609, more than twenty years after the first appearance of Tasso's Jerusalem.——One of the most amiable peculiarities in the character of Lope de Vega, is the extreme liberality with which he commends the merit of his rivals. In his Laurel de Apolo, he celebrates all the eminent Spanish and Portugueze Poets; he speaks both of Camoens and Ercilla with the warmest applause. Among the most pleasing passages in this poem, is a compliment which he pays to his father, who was, like the father of Tasso, a Poet of considerable talents.

Among the smaller pieces of Lope de Vega, there are two particularly curious: a descriptive poem on the garden of his patron the Duke of Alva; and a sonnet in honour of the Invincible Armada. The latter may be considered as a complete model of Spanish bombast: " Go forth and burn the world," says the Poet, addressing himself to that mighty fleet; "my sighs will furnish your sails with a never-failing wind; and my breast will supply your cannon with inexhaustible fire."—— Perhaps this may be equalled by a Spanish character of our Poet, with which I shall close my imperfect account of him. It is his friend and biographer Montalvan, who, in the opening of his life, bestows on him the following titles: El Doctor Frey Lope Felix de Vega Carpio, Portento del Orbe, Gloria de la Nacion, Lustre de la Patria, Oracula de la Lengua, Centro de la Fama, Assumpio de la Invidia, Cuydado de la Fortuna, Fenix de los Siglos, Principe de los Versos, Orfeo de las Ciencias, Apolo de las Musas, Horacio de los Poetas, Virgilio de los Epicos, Homero de los Heroycos, Pindaro de los Lyricos, Sofocles de los Tragicos, y Terencio de los Comicos, Unico entre los Mayores, Mayor entre los Grandes, y Grande a todas Luzes, y en todas Materias.

NOTE X. VERSE 239.

The brave Ercilla sounds, with potent breath,
His Epic trumpet in the fields of death,] Don Alonzo de Ercilla y Zuniga was equally distinguished as a Hero and a Poet; but this exalted character, notwithstanding his double claim to our regard,

regard, is almost totally unknown in our country; and I shall therefore endeavour to give the English reader the best idea that I can, both of his gallant life, and of his singular poem. —He was born in Madrid, on the 7th of August 1533, the third son of Fortun Garcia de Ercilla, who, tho' descended from a noble family, pursued the profession of the law, and was so remarkable for his talents, that he acquired the appellation of " The subtle Spaniard." The mother of our Poet was also noble, and from her he inherited his second title, Zuniga; Ercilla was the name of an ancient castle in Biscay, which had been long in the possession of his paternal ancestors. He lost his father while he was yet an infant; a circumstance which had great influence on his future life: for his mother was received, after the decease of her husband, into the household of the Empress Isabella, the wife of Charles the Vth, and had thus an early opportunity of introducing our young Alonzo into the palace. He soon obtained an appointment there, in the character of page to the Infant Don Philip, to whose service he devoted himself with the most heroic enthusiasm, though Philip was a master who little deserved so generous an attachment. At the age of fourteen, he attended that Prince in the splendid progress which he made, at the desire of his Imperial father,

through

through the principal cities of the Netherlands, and through parts of Italy and Germany. This singular expedition is very circumstantially recorded in a folio volume, by a Spanish historian named Juan Chriftoval Calvete de Eftrella, whose work affords a very curious and ftriking picture of the manners and ceremonies of that martial and romantic age. All the cities which were visited by the Prince contended with each other in magnificent feftivity: the brilliant feries of literary and warlike pageants which they exhibited, though they anfwered not their defign of conciliating the affection of the fullen Philip, might probably awaken the genius of our youthful Poet, and excite his ambition to acquire both poetical and military fame. In 1551, he returned with the Prince into Spain, and continued there for three years; at the end of which he attended his royal mafter to England, on his marriage with Queen Mary, which was celebrated at Winchefter in the fummer of 1554. At this period Ercilla firft affumed the military character; for his fovereign received advice, during his refidence at London, that the martial natives of Arauco, a diftrict on the coaft of Chile, had revolted from the Spanifh government; and difpatched an experienced officer, named Alderete, who attended him in England, to fubdue

the

the infurrection, invefting him with the command of the rebellious province. Ercilla embarked with Alderete; but that officer dying in his paffage, our Poet proceeded to Lima. Don Hurtado de Mendoza, who commanded there as Viceroy of Peru, appointed his fon Don Garcia to fupply the place of Alderete, and fent him with a confiderable force to oppofe the Araucanians. Ercilla was engaged in this enterprize, and greatly diftinguifhed himfelf in the obftinate conteft which enfued. The noble character of the Barbarians who maintained this unequal ftruggle, and the many fplendid feats of valour which this fcene afforded, led our author to the fingular defign of making the war, in which he was himfelf engaged, the fubject of an Heroic poem; which he intitled " La Araucana," from the name of the country. As many of his own particular adventures may be found in the following fummary of his work, I fhall not here enlarge on his military exploits; but proceed to one of the moft mortifying events of his life, which he briefly mentions in the conclufion of his poem. After paffing with great honour through many and various perils, he was on the point of fuffering a difgraceful death, from the rafh orders of his young and inconfiderate Commander. On his return, from an expedition of adventure and difcovery, to the Spanish city of Imperial, he was present at a scene of public festivity displayed there to celebrate the accession of Philip the IId to the crown of Spain. At a kind of tournament, there arose an idle dispute between Ercilla and Don Juan de Pineda, in the heat of which the two disputants drew their swords; many of the spectators joined in the broil; and a report arising that the quarrel was a mere pretence to conceal some mutinous design, the hasty Don Garcia, their General, committed the two antagonists to prison, and sentenced them both to be publicly beheaded. Ercilla himself declares, he was conducted to the scaffold before his precipitate judge discovered the iniquity of the sentence; but his innocence appeared just time enough to save him; and he sems to have been fully reinstated in the good opinion of Don Garcia, as, among the complimentary sonnets addressed to Ercilla, there is one which bears the name of his General, in which he styles him the Divine Alonzo, and celebrates both his military and poetical genius. But Ercilla seems to have been deeply wounded by this affront; for, quitting Chile, he went to Callao, the port of Lima, and there embarked on an expedition against a Spanish rebel, named Lope de Aguirre, who, having murdered his captain, and usurped the chief power, was perpetrating the most

cruel

THIRD EPISTLE.

cruel enormities in the settlement of Venezuela. But Ercilla learned, on his arrival at Panama, that this barbarous usurper was destroyed; he therefore resolved, as his health was much impaired by the hardships he had passed, to return to Spain. He arrived there in the twenty-ninth year of his age; but soon left it, and travelled, as he himself informs us, through France, Italy, Germany, Silesia, Moravia, and Pannonia; but the particulars of this expedition are unknown. In the year 1570 he appeared again at Madrid, and was married to Maria Bazan, a lady whom he contrives to celebrate in the course of his military poem. He is said to have been afterwards gentleman of the bed-chamber to the Emperor Rodolph the IId, a prince who had been educated at Madrid: but the connection of our Poet with this Monarch is very indistinctly recorded; and indeed all the latter part of his life is little known. In the year 1580 he resided at Madrid, in a state of retirement and poverty. The time and circumstances of his death are uncertain: it is proved that he was living in the year 1596, by the evidence of a Spanish writer named Mosquera, who, in a treatise of military discipline, speaks of Ercilla as engaged at that time in celebrating the victories of Don Alvaro Bazan, Marques de Santa Cruz, in a poem which has never appeared, and is

supposed

supposed to have been left imperfect at his death. Some anecdotes related of our Poet afford us ground to hope that his various merits were not entirely unrewarded. It is said, that in speaking to his sovereign Philip, he was so overwhelmed by diffidence that language failed him: " Don Alonzo!" replied the King, " speak to me in writing." He did so, and obtained his request.—The Spanish Historian Ovalle, who has written an account of Chile, in which he frequently supports his narration by the authority of Ercilla, affirms that our Poet presented his work to Philip with his own hand, and received a recompence from the King. But in this circumstance I fear the Historian was mistaken, as he supposes it to have happened on the return of Ercilla from Chile; and our Poet, in a distinct portion of his work, which was not published till many years after that period, expressly declares, in addressing himself to Philip, that all his attempts to serve him had been utterly unrequited. Ercilla left no legitimate family; but had some natural children, the most eminent of which was a daughter, who was advantageously married to a nobleman of Portugal.

In that elegant collection of Spanish Poets, " *Parnaso Espanol*," there is a pleasing little amorous poem, written by Ercilla in his youth,
which

which is peculiarly commended by Lope de Vega; who has bestowed a very generous encomium on our Poet, in his " *Laurel de Apolo.*" But the great and singular work which has justly rendered Ercilla immortal, is his Poem intitled Araucana, which was published in three separate parts: the first appeared in 1577; he added the second in the succeeding year; and in 1590 he printed a complete edition of the whole. It was applauded by the most eminent writers of Spain; and Cervantes, in speaking of Don Quixote's Library, has ranked it among the choicest treasures of the Castilian Muse. Voltaire, who speaks of Ercilla with his usual spirit and inaccuracy, has the merit of having made our Poet more generally known, though his own acquaintance with him appears to have been extremely slight; for he affirms that Ercilla was in the battle of Saint Quintin: a mistake into which he never could have fallen, had he read the Araucana. Indeed the undistinguishing censure which he passes on the poem in general, after commending one particular passage, sufficiently proves him a perfect stranger to many subsequent parts of the work; yet his remark on the inequality of the Poet is just. Ercilla is certainly unequal; but, with all his defects, he appears to me one of the most extraordinary

traordinary and engaging characters in the poetical world. Perhaps I am a little partial to him, from the accidental circumstance of having first read his poem with a departed friend, whose opinions are very dear to me, and who was particularly fond of this military Bard. However this may be, my idea of Ercilla's merit has led me to hazard the following extensive sketch of his work:—it has swelled to a much larger size than I at first intended; for I was continually tempted to extend it, by the desire of not injuring the peculiar excellencies of this wonderful Poet. If I have not utterly failed in that desire, the English reader will be enabled to judge and to enjoy an author, who, considering his subject and its execution, may be said to stand single and unparalleled in the host of Poets. His beauties and his defects are of so obvious a nature, that I shall not enlarge upon them; but let it be remembered, that his poem was composed amidst the toils and perils of the most fatiguing and hazardous service, and that his verses were sometimes written on scraps of leather, from the want of better materials. His style is remarkably pure and perspicuous; and, notwithstanding the restraint of rhyme, it has frequently all the ease, the spirit, and the volubility of Homer. I wish not, however,

ever, to conceal his defects; and I have therefore given a very fair account of the strange episode he introduces concerning the history of Dido, which has justly fallen under the ridicule of Voltaire. I must however observe, as an apology for Ercilla, that many Bards of his country have considered it as a point of honour to defend the reputation of this injured lady, and to attack Virgil with a kind of poetical Quixotism for having slandered the chastity of so spotless a heroine. If my memory does not deceive me, both Lope de Vega and Quevedo have employed their pens as the champions of Dido. We may indeed very readily join the laugh of the lively Frenchman against our Poet on this occasion; but let us recollect that Ercilla has infinitely more Homeric spirit, and that his poem contains more genuine Epic beauties, than can be found in Voltaire.

Ercilla has been honoured with many poetical encomiums by the writers of his own country; and, as I believe the most elegant compliment which has been paid to his genius is the production of a Spanish lady, I shall close this account of him with a translation of the Sonnet, in which she celebrates both the Hero and the Poet.

SONETO

SONETO

DE LA SEÑORA DOÑA LEONOR DE ICIZ,
SEÑORA DE LA BARONIA DE RAFALES
A DON ALONSO DE ERCILLA.

Mil bronces para eftatuas ya forxados,
Mil lauros de tus obras premio honrofo
Te ofrece Efpaña, Ercilla generofo,
Por tu pluma y tu lanza tan ganados.
Hourefe tu valor entre foldados,
Invidie tu nobleza el valerofo,
Y bufque en tí el poeta mas famofo
Lima para fus verfos mas limados.
Derrame por el mundo tus loores
La fama, y eternice tu memoria,
Porque jamás el tiempo la confuma.
Gocen ya, fin temor de que hay mayores
Tus hechos, y tus libros de igual gloria,
Pues la han ganado igual la efpada y pluma.

SONNET

FROM THE LADY LEONORA DE ICIZ,
BARONESS OF RAFALES,
TO DON ALONZO DE ERCILLA.

Marble, that forms the Hero's mimic frame,
And laurels, that reward the Poet's strain,
Accept, Ercilla, from thy grateful Spain!
Thy sword and pen alike this tribute claim.
Our Warriors honour thy heroic name;
Thy birth is envy'd by Ambition's train;
Thy verses teach the Bard of happiest vein
A finer polish, and a nobler aim.
May glory round the world thy merit spread!
In Memory's volume may thy praises stand,
In characters that time shall ne'er destroy!
Thy songs, and thy exploits, without the dread
To be surpass'd by a superior hand,
With equal right their equal fame enjoy!

A SKETCH

A SKETCH OF THE ARAUCANA.

THE Poem of Ercilla opens with the following expofition of his fubject:

I Sing not love of ladies, nor of fights
   Devis'd for gentle dames by courteous knights;
Nor feafts, nor tourneys, nor that tender care
Which prompts the Gallant to regale the Fair;
But the bold deeds of Valour's fav'rite train,
Thofe undegenerate fons of warlike Spain,
Who made Arauco their ftern laws embrace,
And bent beneath their yoke her untam'd race,
Of tribes diftinguifh'd in the field I fing;
Of nations who difdain the name of King;
Courage, that danger only taught to grow,
And challenge honour from a generous foe;
And perfevering toils of pureft fame,
And feats that aggrandize the Spanifh name:
For the brave actions of the vanquifh'd fpread
The brighteft glory round the victor's head.

He then addreffes his work to his fovereign, Philip the Second, and devotes his firft Canto to the defcription of that part of the New World which forms the fcene of his action, and is called Arauco;
                                       a diftrict

THIRD EPISTLE.

a diſtrict in the province of Chile. He paints the ſingular character and various cuſtoms of its warlike inhabitants with great clearneſs and ſpirit. In many points they bear a ſtriking reſemblance to the ancient Germans, as they are drawn with a kind of poetical energy by the ſtrong pencil of Tacitus. The firſt Canto cloſes with a brief account how this martial province was ſubdued by a Spaniſh officer named Valdivia; with an intimation that his negligence in his new dominion gave birth to thoſe important exploits which the Poet propoſes to celebrate.

CANTO II.

ERCILLA begins his Cantos much in the manner of Arioſto, with a moral reflection; ſometimes rather too much dilated, but generally expreſſed in eaſy, elegant, and ſpirited verſe.—The following lines faintly imitate the two firſt ſtanzas of his ſecond Canto:

Many there are who, in this mortal ſtrife,
Have reach'd the ſlippery heights of ſplendid life:
For Fortune's ready hand its ſuccour lent;
Smiling ſhe rais'd them up the ſteep aſcent,

To

> To hurl them headlong from that lofty feat
> To which she led their unsuspecting feet;
> E'en at the moment when all fears disperse,
> And their proud fancy sees no sad reverse.
> Little they think, beguil'd by fair success,
> That Joy is but the herald of Distress:
> The hasty wing of Time escapes their sight,
> And those dark evils that attend his flight:
> Vainly they dream, with gay presumption warm,
> Fortune for them will take a steadier form;
> She, unconcern'd at what her victims feel,
> Turns with her wonted haste her fatal wheel.

After blaming his countrymen for abusing their good fortune, the Poet celebrates, in the following spirited manner, the eagerness and indignation with which the Indians prepared to wreak their vengeance on their Spanish oppressors:

> The Indians first, by novelty dismay'd,
> As Gods rever'd us, and as Gods obey'd;
> But when they found we were of woman born,
> Their homage turn'd to enmity and scorn:
> Their childish error when our weakness show'd,
> They blush'd at what their ignorance bestow'd;
> Fiercely they burnt with anger and with shame,
> To see their masters but of mortal frame.

Disdaining

THIRD EPISTLE.

Difdaining cold and cowardly delay,
They feek atonement, on no diftant day:
Prompt and refolv'd, in quick debate they join,
To form of deep revenge their dire defign.
Impatient that their bold decree fhould fpread,
And fhake the world around with fudden dread,
Th' affembling Chieftains led fo large a train,
Their ready hoft o'erfpread th' extenfive plain.
No fummons now the foldier's heart requires,
The thirft of battle every breaft infpires;
No pay, no promife of reward, they afk,
Keen to accomplifh their fpontaneous tafk;
And, by the force of one avenging blow,
Crufh and annihilate their foreign foe.
Of fome brave Chiefs, who to this council came,
Well may'ft thou, Memory, preferve the name;
Tho' rude and favage, yet of noble foul,
Juftly they claim their place on Glory's roll,
Who robbing Spain of many a gallant fon,
In fo confin'd a fpace fuch victories won;
Whofe fame fome living Spaniards yet may fpread,
Too well attefted by our warlike dead.

The Poet proceeds to mention, in the manner of Homer, but in a much fhorter catalogue, the principal Chieftains, and the number of their refpective vaffals.

Uncouthly as their names muſt found to an Engliſh ear, it ſeems neceſſary to run through the liſt, as theſe free and noble-minded ſavages act ſo diſtinguiſhed a part in the courſe of the poem. —Tucapel ſtands firſt; renowned for the moſt inveterate enmity to the Chriſtians, and leader of three thouſand vaſſals: Angol, a valiant youth, attended by four thouſand: Cayocupil, with three; and Millarapue, an elder chief, with five thouſand: Paycabi, with three thouſand; and Lemolemo, with ſix: Maregnano, Gualèmo, and Lebopia, with three thouſand each: Elicura, diſtinguiſhed by ſtrength of body and deteſtation of ſervitude, with ſix thouſand; and the ancient Colocolo with a ſuperior number: Ongolmo, with four thouſand; and Puren, with ſix: the fierce and gigantic Lincoya with a ſtill larger train. Peteguelen, lord of the valley of Arauco, prevented from perſonal attendance by the Chriſtians, diſpatches ſix thouſand of his retainers to the aſſembly: the moſt diſtinguiſhed of his party are Thomè and Andalican. The Lord of the maritime province of Pilmayquen, the bold Caupolican, is alſo unable to appear at the opening of the council. Many other Chieftains attended, whoſe names the Poet ſuppreſſes, leſt his prolixity ſhould offend. As they begin their buſineſs in the ſtyle of the ancient Germans,

THIRD EPISTLE.

Germans, with a plentiful banquet, they soon grow exasperated with liquor, and a violent quarrel ensues concerning the command of the forces for the projected war: an honour which almost every Chieftain was arrogant enough to challenge for himself. In the midst of this turbulent debate, the ancient Colocolo delivers the following harangue, which Voltaire prefers (and I think with great justice) to the speech of Nestor, on a similar occasion, in the first Iliad:

Assembled Chiefs! ye guardians of the land!
Think not I mourn from thirst of lost command,
To find your rival spirits thus pursue
A post of honour which I deem my due.
These marks of age, you see, such thoughts disown
In me, departing for the world unknown;
But my warm love, which ye have long possest,
Now prompts that counsel which you'll find the best.
Why should we now for marks of glory jar?
Why wish to spread our martial name afar?
Crush'd as we are by Fortune's cruel stroke,
And bent beneath an ignominious yoke,
Ill can our minds such noble pride maintain,
While the fierce Spaniard holds our galling chain.
Your generous fury here ye vainly shew;
Ah! rather pour it on th' embattled foe!

What frenzy has your fouls of fenfe bereav'd?
Ye rufh to felf-perdition, unperceiv'd.
'Gainft your own vitals would ye lift thofe hands,
Whofe vigour ought to burft oppreffion's bands?
   If a defire of death this rage create,
O die not yet in this difgraceful ftate!
Turn your keen arms, and this indignant flame,⎫
Againft the breaft of thofe who fink your fame, ⎬
Who made the world a witnefs of your fhame. ⎭
Hafte ye to caft thefe hated bonds away,
In this the vigour of your fouls difplay;
Nor blindly lavifh, from your country's veins,
Blood that may yet redeem her from her chains.
   E'en while I thus lament, I ftill admire
The fervour of your fouls; they give me fire:
But juftly trembling at their fatal bent,
I dread fome dire calamitous event;
Left in your rage Diffenfion's frantic hand
Should cut the finews of our native land.
If fuch its doom, my thread of being burft,
And let your old compeer expire the firft!
Shall this fhrunk frame, thus bow'd by age's weight,
Live the weak witnefs of a nation's fate?
No: let fome friendly fword, with kind relief,
Forbid its finking in that fcene of grief.
Happy whofe eyes in timely darknefs clofe,
Sav'd from that worft of fights, his country's woes!
                                                  Yet,

Yet, while I can, I make your weal my care,
And for the public good my thoughts declare.
 Equal ye are in courage and in worth;
Heaven has assign'd to all an equal birth:
In wealth, in power, and majesty of soul,
Each Chief seems worthy of the world's controul.
These gracious gifts, not gratefully beheld,
To this dire strife your daring minds impell'd.
 But on your generous valour I depend,
That all our country's woes will swiftly end.
A Leader still our present state demands,
To guide to vengeance our impatient bands;
Fit for this hardy task that Chief I deem,
Who longest may sustain a massive beam:
Your rank is equal, let your force be try'd,
And for the strongest let his strength decide.

 The Chieftains acquiesce in this proposal; which, as Voltaire justly observes, is very natural in a nation of savages. The beam is produced, and of a size so enormous, that the Poet declares himself afraid to specify its weight. The first Chieftains who engage in the trial support it on their shoulders five and six hours each; Tucapel fourteen; and Lincoya more than double that number; when the assembly, considering his strength as almost supernatural, is eager to bestow on him

H 3   the

the title of General: but in the moment he is exulting in this new honour, Caupolican arrives without attendants. His perfon and character are thus defcribed by the Poet:

> Tho' from his birth one darken'd eye he drew
> (The viewlefs orb was of the granite's hue),
> Nature, who partly robb'd him of his fight,
> Repaid this failure by redoubled might.
> This noble youth was of the higheft ftate;
> His actions honour'd, and his words of weight:
> Prompt and refolv'd in every generous caufe,
> A friend to Juftice and her fterneft laws:
> Fafhion'd for fudden feats, or toils of length,
> His limbs poffefs'd both fupplenefs and ftrength:
> Dauntlefs his mind, determin'd and adroit·
> In every quick and hazardous exploit.

This accomplifhed Chieftain is received with great joy by the affembly; and, having furpaffed Lincoya by many degrees in the trial, is invefted with the fupreme command. He difpatches a fmall party to attack a neighbouring Spanifh fort: they execute his orders, and make a vigorous affault. After a fharp conflict they are repulfed; but in the moment of their retreat Caupolican arrives with his army to their fupport. The Spaniards in defpair evacuate

evacuate the fort, and make their escape in the night: the news is brought to Valdivia, the Spanish Commander in the city of Concepcion;—and with his resolution to punish the Barbarians the canto concludes.

CANTO III.

O CURELESS malady! Oh fatal pest!
 Embrac'd with ardour and with pride carest;
Thou common vice, thou most contagious ill,
Bane of the mind, and frenzy of the will!
Thou foe to private and to public health;
Thou dropsy of the soul, that thirsts for wealth,
Insatiate Avarice!—'tis from thee we trace
The various misery of our mortal race.

With this spirited and generous invective against that prevailing vice of his countrymen, which sullied the lustre of their most brilliant exploits, Ercilla opens his 3d canto. He does not scruple to assert, that the enmity of the Indians arose from the avaricious severity of their Spanish oppressors; and he accuses Valdivia on this head, though he gives him the praise of a brave and gallant officer. ——This Spaniard, on the first intelligence of the Indian infurrection, difpatched his fcouts from the city where he commanded. They do not return. Preffed by the impatient gallantry of his trooops, Valdivia marches out;—they foon difcover the mangled heads of his meffengers fixed up as a fpectacle of terror on the road. Valdivia deliberates what meafures to purfue. His army entreat him to continue his march. He confents, being piqued by their infinuations of his difgracing the Spanifh arms. An Indian ally brings him an account that twenty thoufand of the confederated Indians are waiting to deftroy him in the valley of Tucapel. He ftill preffes forward; arrives in fight of the fort which the Indians had deftroyed, and engages them in a moft obftinate battle; in the defcription of which, the Poet introduces an original and ftriking fimile, in the following manner:

The fteady pikemen of the favage band,
Waiting our hafty charge, in order ftand;
But when th' advancing Spaniard aim'd his ftroke,
Their ranks, to form a hollow fquare, they broke;
An eafy paffage to our troop they leave,
And deep within their lines their foes receive;
Their files refuming then the ground they gave,
Bury the Chriftians in that clofing grave.

As

THIRD EPISTLE.

As the keen Crocodile, who loves to lay
His silent ambush for his finny prey,
Hearing the scaly tribe with sportive sound
Advance, and cast a muddy darkness round,
Opens his mighty mouth, with caution, wide,
And, when th' unwary fish within it glide,
Closing with eager haste his hollow jaw,
Thus satiates with their lives his rav'nous maw:
So, in their toils, without one warning thought,
The murd'rous foe our little squadron caught
With quick destruction, in a fatal strife,
From whence no Christian soldier 'scap'd with life.

Such was the fate of the advanced guard of the Spaniards. The Poet then describes the conflict of the main army with great spirit :—ten Spaniards distinguish themselves by signal acts of courage, but are all cut in pieces. The battle proceeds thus;

The hostile sword, now deeply dy'd in blood,
Drench'd the wide field with many a sanguine flood;
Courage still grows to form the fierce attack,
But wasted vigour makes the combat slack:
No pause they seek, to gain exhausted breath,
No rest, except the final rest of death:
The wariest combatants now only try
To snatch the sweets of vengeance ere they die.

The

The fierce difdain of death, and fcorn of flight,
Give to our fcanty troop fuch wond'rous might,
The Araucanian hoft begin to yield;
They quit with lofs and fhame the long-fought
  field:
They fly; and their purfuers fhake the plain
With joyous fhouts of Victory and Spain.
But dire mifchance, and Fate's refiftlefs fway,
Gave a ftrange iffue to the dreadful day.
  An Indian Youth, a noble Chieftain's fon,
Who as our friend his martial feats begun,
Our Leader's Page, by him to battle train'd,
Who now befide him the hard fight fuftain'd,
As he beheld his kindred Chiefs retire,
Felt an indignant flafh of Patriot fire;
And thus incited to a glorious ftand
The flying champions of his native land:
  Mifguided Country! by vain fear pofleft,
Ah whither doft thou turn thy timid breaft?
Ye brave compatriots, fhall your ancient fame
Be vilely buried in this field of fhame?
Thofe laws, thofe rights, ye gloried to defend,
All perifh, all, by this ignoble end!
From Chiefs of dreaded power, and honour'd worth,
Ye fink to abject flaves, the fcorn of earth!
To the pure founders of your boafted race
Ye give the curelefs wound of deep difgrace!
                                        Behold

THIRD EPISTLE.

Behold the wasted vigour of your foe!
See, bath'd in sweat and blood, their coursers blow!
Lose not your mental force, your martial fires,
Our best inheritance from generous sires;
Sink not the noble Araucanian name
From glory's summit to the depths of shame;
Fly, fly the servitude your souls detest!
To the keen sword oppose the dauntless breast.
Why shew ye frames endued with manly power,
Yet shrink from danger in the trying hour?
Fix in your minds the friendly truth I speak;
Vain are your fears, your terror blind and weak:
Now make your names immortal; now restore
Freedom's lost blessings to your native shore:
Now turn, while Fame and Victory invite,
While prosp'rous Fortune calls you to the fight;
Or yet a moment cease, O cease to fly,
And for our country learn of me to die!

   As thus he speaks, his eager steps advance,
And 'gainst the Spanish Chief he points his lance;
To lead his kindred fugitives from flight,
Singly he dares to tempt th' unequal fight:
Against our circling arms, that round him shine,
Eager he darts amidst the thickest line,
Keen as, when chaf'd by summer's fiery beam,
The young Stag plunges in the cooling stream.

The

NOTES TO THE

The Poet proceeds to relate the great agility and valour displayed by Lautaro, for such is the name of this gallant and patriotic Youth: and, as Ercilla has a foul sufficiently heroic to do full justice to the virtues of an enemy, he gives him the highest praise. Having mentioned on the occasion many heroes of ancient history, he exclaims:

Say, of these famous Chiefs can one exceed
Or match this young Barbarian's noble deed?
Vict'ry for them, her purpose unexplor'd,
Tempted by equal chance their happy sword:
What risk, what peril, did they boldly meet,
Save where Ambition urg'd the splendid feat;
Or mightier Int'rest fir'd the daring mind,
Which makes a Hero of the fearful Hind?
Many there are who with a brave disdain
Face all the perils of the deathful plain,
Who, fir'd by hopes of glory, nobly dare,
Yet fail the stroke of adverse chance to bear;
With animated fire their spirit shines,
Till the short splendor of their day declines;
But all their valour, all their strength expires,
When fickle Fortune from their side retires.
This youthful Hero, when the die was cast,
War's dire decree against his country past,

Made

THIRD EPISTLE.

Made the stern Power the finish'd cause resume,
And finally reverse the cruel doom:
He, by his efforts in the dread debate,
Forc'd the determin'd will of adverse Fate;
From shouting Triumph rush'd the palm to tear,
And fix'd it on the brow of faint Despair.

Caupolican, leading his army back to the charge in consequence of Lautaro's efforts in their favour, obtains a complete victory. The Spaniards are all slain in the field, except their Commander Valdivia, who flies, attended only by a priest; but he is soon taken prisoner, and conducted before the Indian Chief, who is inclined to spare his life; when an elder savage, called Leocato, in a sudden burst of indignation, kills him with his club.

All the people of Arauco assemble in a great plain to celebrate their victory: old and young, women and children, unite in the festival; and the trees that surround the scene of their assembly are decorated with the heads and spoils of their slaughtered enemies.

They meditate the total extermination of the Spaniards from their country, and even a descent on Spain. The General makes a prudent speech to restrain their impetuosity; and afterwards, be-
stowing

stowing just applause on the brave exploit of the young Lautaro, appoints him his lieutenant. In the midst of the festivity, Caupolican receives advice that a party of fourteen Spanish horsemen had attacked some of his forces with great havoc. He dispatches Lautaro to oppose them.

CANTO IV.

A PARTY of fourteen gallant Spaniards, who had set forth from the city of Imperial to join Valdivia, not being apprised of his unhappy fate, are surprised by the enemy where they expected to meet their Commander;—they defend themselves with great valour. They are informed by a friendly Indian of the fate of Valdivia. They attempt to retreat; but are surrounded by numbers of the Araucanians:—when the Poet introduces the following instance of Spanish heroism, which I insert as a curious stroke of their military character:

Here, cried a Spaniard, far unlike his race,
Nor shall his abject name my verse debase,
Marking his few associates march along,
O that our band were but a hundred strong!

The brave Gonsalo with disdain replied:
Rather let two be sever'd from our side,
Kind Heaven! that Memory may our feats proclaim,
And call our little troop The Twelve of Fame!

They continue to fight with great bravery against superior numbers, when Lautaro arrives with a fresh army against them. Still undaunted, they only resolve to sell their lives as dear as possible. Seven of them are cut to pieces.—In the midst of the slaughter a furious thunder and hail storm arises, by which incident the surviving seven escape. The tempest is described with the following original simile:

Now in the turbid air a stormy cloud
Spreads its terrific shadow o'er the crowd;
The gathering darkness hides the solar ray,
And to th' affrighted earth denies the day;
The rushing winds, to which the forests yield,
Rive the tall tree, and desolate the field:
In drops distinct and rare now falls the rain;
And now with thickening fury beats the plain.
As the bold master of the martial drum,
Ere to the shock th' advancing armies come,
In aweful notes, that shake the heaven's high arch,
Intrepid strikes the slow and solemn march;
But,

But, when the charging heroes yield their breath,
Doubles the horrid harmony of death:
So the dark tempest, with increasing sound,
Pours the loud deluge on the echoing ground.

The few Spaniards that escape take refuge in a neighbouring fort; which they abandon the following day on hearing the fate of Valdivia. Lautaro returns, and receives new honours and new forces from his General, to march against a Spanish army, which departs from the city of Penco under the command of Villagran, an experienced officer, to revenge the death of Valdivia. The departure of the troops from Penco is described, and the distress of the women.—Villagran marches with expedition towards the frontiers of Arauco. He arrives at a dangerous pass, and finds Lautaro, with his army of 10,100 Indians, advantageously posted on the heights, and waiting with great steadiness and discipline to give him battle.

CANTO V.

LAUTARO with great difficulty restrains the eager Indians in their post on the rock. He suffers a few to descend and skirmish on the lower ground, where several distinguish themselves in

single

THIRD EPISTLE.

single combat. The Spaniards attempt in vain to dislodge the army of Lautaro by an attack of their cavalry:—they afterwards fire on them from six pieces of cannon.

The vext air feels the thunder of the fight,
And smoke and flame involve the mountain's height;
Earth seems to open as the flames aspire,
And new volcano's spout destructive fire.
 Lautaro saw no hopes of life allow'd,
Save by dispersing this terrific cloud,
That pours its lightning with so dire a shock,
Smiting his lessen'd host, who strew the rock;
And to the troop of Leucoton the brave
His quick command the skilful Leader gave:
He bids them fiercely to the charge descend,
And thus exhorts aloud each ardent friend:
 My faithful partners in bright victory's meed,
Whom fortune summons to this noble deed,
Behold the hour when your prevailing might
Shall prove that Justice guards us in the fight!
Now firmly fix your lances in the rest,
And rush to honour o'er each hostile breast;
Through every bar your bloody passage force,
Nor let a brother's fall impede your course;
Be yon dread instruments of death your aim;
Possest of these you gain eternal fame:

Vol. IV.   I   The

The camp shall follow your triumphant trace,
And own you leaders in the glorious chace.
  While these bold words their ardent zeal exalt,
They rush impetuous to the rash assault.

  The Indians, undismayed by a dreadful slaughter, gain possession of the cannon.—Villagran makes a short but spirited harangue to his flying soldiers. He is unable to rally them: and, chusing rather to die than to survive so ignominious a defeat, rushes into the thickest of the enemy:—when the Poet, leaving his fate uncertain, concludes the canto.

CANTO VI.

THE valiant mind is privileg'd to feel
    Superior to each turn of Fortune's wheel:
Chance has no power its value to debase,
Or brand it with the mark of deep disgrace:
So thought the noble Villagran, our Chief,
Who chose that death should end his present grief,
And smooth the horrid path, with thorns o'erspread,
Which Destiny condemn'd his feet to tread.

  With the preceding encomium on the spirit of this unfortunate officer the Poet opens his 6th Canto.

Canto. Thirteen of the moſt faithful ſoldiers of Villagran, perceiving their Leader fallen motionleſs under the fury of his enemies, make a deſperate effort to preſerve him.—Being placed again on his horſe by theſe generous deliverers, he recovers from the blow which had ſtunned him; and by ſingular exertion, with the aſſiſtance of his ſpirited little troop, effects his eſcape, and rejoins his main army; whom he endeavours in vain to lead back againſt the triumphant Araucanians. The purſuit becomes general, and the Poet deſcribes the horrid maſſacre committed by the Indians on all the unhappy fugitives that fell into their hands. —The Spaniards in their flight are ſtopt by a narrow paſs fortified and guarded by a party of Indians. Villagran forces the rude entrenchment in perſon, and conducts part of his army ſafe through the paſs; but many, attempting other roads over the mountainous country, are either loſt among the precipices of the rocks, or purſued and killed by the Indians.

CANTO VII.

THE remains of the Spaniſh army, after infinite loſs and fatigue, at laſt reach the city of Concepcion.

Their entrance in these walls let fancy paint,
O'erwhelm'd with anguish, and with labour faint:
These gash'd with ghastly wounds, those writh'd
　　with pain,
And some their human semblance scarce retain;
They seem unhappy spirits 'scap'd from hell,
Yet wanting voice their misery to tell.
Their pangs to all their rolling eyes express,
And silence most declares their deep distress.

When weariness and shame at length allow'd
Their tongues to satisfy th' enquiring crowd,
From the pale citizens, amaz'd to hear
A tale surpassing e'en their wildest fear,
One general sound of lamentation rose,
That deeply solemniz'd a nation's woes;
The neighbouring mansions to their grief reply,
And every wall return'd the mournful cry.

　　The inhabitants of Concepcion, expecting every instant the triumphant Lautaro at their gates, resolve to abandon their city. A gallant veteran upbraids their cowardly design. They disregard his reproaches, and evacuate the place:—when the Poet introduces the following instance of female heroism:

'Tis just that Fame a noble deed display,
Which claims remembrance, even to the day

　　　　　　　　　　　　　　When

When Memory's hand no more the pen shall use,
But sink in darkness, and her being lose:
The lovely Mencia, an accomplish'd Dame,
A valiant spirit in a tender frame,
Here firmly shew'd, as this dread scene began,
Courage now found not in the heart of man.
The bed of sickness 'twas her chance to press;
But when she heard the city's loud distress,
Snatching such weapons as the time allow'd,
She rush'd indignant midst the flying crowd.

   Now up the neighbouring hill they slowly wind,
And, bending oft their mournful eyes behind,
Cast a sad look, of every hope bereft,
On those rich plains, the precious home they left.

   More poignant grief see generous Mencia feel,
More noble proof she gives of patriot zeal:
Waving a sword in her heroic hand,
In their tame march she stopt the timid band;
Cross'd the ascending road before their van,
And, turning to the city, thus began:

   Thou valiant nation, whose unequall'd toils
Have dearly purchas'd fame and golden spoils,
Where is the courage ye so oft display'd
Against this foe, from whom ye shrink dismay'd?
Where those high hopes, and that aspiring flame,
Which made immortal praise your constant aim?

Where your firm fouls, that every chance defied,
And native ftrength, that form'd your noble pride?
Ah whither would you fly, in felfifh fear,
In frantic hafte, with no purfuer near?
 How oft has cenfure to your hearts affign'd
Ardor too keenly brave and rafhly blind;
Eager to dart amid the doubtful fray,
Scorning the ufeful aid of wife delay?
Have we not feen you with contempt oppofe,
And bend beneath your yoke unnumber'd foes;
Attempt and execute defigns fo bold,
Ye grew immortal as ye heard them told?
 Turn! to your people turn a pitying eye,
To whom your fears thefe happy feats deny!
Turn! and furvey this fair this fertile land,
Whofe ready tribute waits your lordly hand;
Survey its pregnant mines, its fands of gold;
Survey the flock now wandering from its fold,
Mark how it vainly feeks, in wild defpair,
The faithlefs fhepherd, who forfakes his care.
 E'en the dumb creatures of domeftic kind,
Though not endow'd with man's difcerning mind,
Now fhew the femblance of a reafoning foul,
And in their mafters' mifery condole:
The ftronger animals, of fterner heart,
Take in this public woe a feeling part;

          Their

Their plantive roar, that speaks their sense aright,
Justly upbraids your ignominious flight.
Ye fly from quiet, opulence, and fame,
Purchas'd by valour, your acknowledg'd claim;
From these ye fly, to seek a foreign seat,
Where dastard fugitives no welcome meet.
How deep the shame, an abject life to spend
In poor dependance on a pitying friend!
Turn!—let the brave their only choice await,
Or honourable life, or instant fate.
    Return! return! O quit this path of shame!
Stain not by fear your yet unsullied name;
Myself I offer, if our foes advance,
To rush the foremost on the hostile lance;
My actions then shall with my words agree,
And what a woman dares your eyes shall see.
Return! return! she cried; but cried in vain;
Her fire seem'd frenzy to the coward train.

    The dastardly inhabitants of the city, unmoved by this remonstrance of the noble Donna Mencia de Nidos, continue their precipitate flight, and, after twelve days of confusion and fatigue, reach the city of Santiago, in the valley of Mapocho. Lautaro arrives in the mean time before the walls they had deserted:—and the Poet concludes his canto with a spirited description of the barbaric fury

fury with which the Indians entered the abandoned city, and deftroyed by fire the rich and magnificent manfions of their Spanifh oppreffors.

CANTO VIII.

LAUTARO is recalled from his victorious exploits, to affift at a general affembly of the Indians, in the valley of Arauco. The different Chieftains deliver their various fentiments concerning the war, after their Leader Caupolican has declared his defign to purfue the Spaniards with unceafing vengeance. The veteran Colocolo propofes a plan for their military operations. An ancient Augur, named Puchecalco, denounces ruin on all the projects of his countrymen, in the name of the Indian Dæmon Eponamon. He recites the omens of their deftruction. The fierce Tucapel, provoked to frenzy by this gloomy prophet, ftrikes him dead in the midft of his harangue, by a fudden blow of his mace. Caupolican orders the murderous Chieftain to be led to inftant death. He defends himfelf with fuccefs againft numbers who attempt to feize him. Lautaro, pleafed by this exertion of his wonderful force and valour, intreats the General to forgive what had paffed; and, at

his

his interceffion, Tucapel is received into favour. Lautaro then clofes the bufinefs of the affembly, by recommending the plan propofed by Colocolo, and intreating that he may himfelf be entrufted with a detached party of five hundred Indians, with which he engages to reduce the city of Santiago. His propofal is accepted. The Chieftains, having finifhed their debate, declare their refolutions to their people; and, after their ufual feftivity, Caupolican, with the main army, proceeds to attack the city of Imperial.

CANTO IX.

THE Poet opens this Canto with an apology for a miracle, which he thinks it neceffary to relate, as it was attefted by the whole Indian army; and, though it does not afford him any very uncommon or fublime imagery, he embellifhes the wonder he defcribes, by his eafy and fpirited verfification, of which the following lines are an imperfect copy:

When to the city's weak defencelefs wall
Its foes were rufhing, at their trumpet's call,
The air grew troubled with portentous found,
And mournful omens multiplied around;

With

With furious fhock the elements engage,
And all the winds contend in all their rage.
From clafhing clouds their mingled torrents gufh,
And rain and hail with rival fury rufh.
Bolts of loud thunder, floods of lightning rend
The opening fkies, and into earth defcend.

O'er the vaft army equal terrors fpread;
No mind efcapes the univerfal dread;
No breaft, tho' arm'd with adamantine power,
Holds its firm vigour in this horrid hour;
For now the fierce Eponamon appears,
And in a Dragon's form augments their fears;
Involving flames around the Dæmon fwell,
Who fpeaks his mandate in a hideous yell:
He bids his votaries with hafte inveft
The trembling city, by defpair depreft.
Where'er th' invading fquadrons force their way,
He promifes their arms an eafy prey.
Spare not (he cry'd) in the relentlefs ftrife,
One Spanifh battlement, one Chriftian life!
He fpoke, and, while the hoft his will adore,
Melts into vapour, and is feen no more.

Quick as he vanifh'd Nature's ftruggles ceafe;
The troubled elements are footh'd to peace:
The winds no longer rage with boundlefs ire,
But, hufh'd in filence, to their caves retire:
The clouds difperfe, reftoring as they fly
The unobftructed fun and azure fky;

Fear

THIRD EPISTLE.

Fear only held its place, and still possest
Usurp'd dominion o'er the boldest breast.

The tempest ceas'd, and heaven, serenely bright,
Array'd the moisten'd earth in joyous light:
When, pois'd upon a cloud that swiftly flew,
A Female form descended to their view,
Clad in the radiance of so rich a veil,
As made the sun's meridian lustre pale;
For it outshone his golden orb as far
As his full blaze outshines the twinkling star.
Her sacred features banish all their dread,
And o'er the host reviving comfort shed.
An hoary Elder by her side appear'd,
For age and sanctity of life rever'd;
And thus she spoke, with soft persuasive grace:
Ah! whither rush ye, blind devoted race?
Turn, while you can, towards your native plain,
Nor 'gainst yon city point your arms in vain;
For God will guard his faithful Christian band,
And give them empire o'er your bleeding land,
Since, thankless, false, and obstinate in ill,
You scorn submission to his sacred will.
Yet shun those walls; th' Almighty, there ador'd,
There arms his people with Destruction's sword.

So spoke the Vision, with an angel's tongue,
And thro' the spacious air to heaven she sprung.

The

The Indians, confounded by this miraculous interpofition, difperfe in diforder to their feveral homes; and the Poet proceeds very gravely to affirm, that, having obtained the beft information, from many individuals, concerning this miracle, that he might be very exact in his account of it, he finds it happened on the twenty-third of April, four years before he wrote the verfes that defcribe it, and in the year of our Lord 1554. The Vifion was followed by peftilence and famine among the Indians. They remain inactive during the winter, but affemble again the enfuing fpring, in the plains of Arauco, to renew the war. They receive intelligence that the Spaniards are attempting to rebuild the city of Concepcion, and are requefted by the neighbouring tribes to march to their affiftance, and prevent that defign. Lautaro leads a chofen band on that expedition, hoping to furprize the fort the Spaniards had erected on the ruins of their city; but the Spanifh commander, Alvarado, being apprized of their motion, fallies forth to meet the Indian party: a fkirmifh enfues; the Spaniards retire to their fort; Lautaro attempts to ftorm it; a moft bloody encounter enfues; Tucapel fignalizes himfelf in the attack; the Indians perfevere with the moft obftinate valour, and, after a long conflict (defcribed with a confiderable

portion

portion of Homeric spirit) gain possession of the fort; Alvarado and a few of his followers escape; they are pursued, and much galled in their flight: a single Indian, named Rengo, harrasses Alvarado and two of his attendants; the Spanish officer, provoked by the insult, turns with his two companions to punish their pursuer; but the wily Indian secures himself on some rocky heights, and annoys them with his sling, till, despairing of revenge, they continue their flight.

CANTO X.

THE Indians celebrate their victory with public games; and prizes are appointed for such as excel in their various martial exercises. Leucoton is declared victor in the contest of throwing the lance, and receives a scimitar as his reward. Rengo subdues his two rivals, Cayeguan and Talco, in the exercise of wrestling, and proceeds to contend with Leucoton. After a long and severe struggle, Rengo has the misfortune to fall by an accidental failure of the ground, but, springing lightly up, engages his adversary with increasing fury; and the canto ends without deciding the contest.

CANTO

NOTES TO THE

CANTO XI.

LAUTARO separates the two enraged antagonists, to prevent the ill effects of their wrath. The youth Orompello, whom Leucoton had before surpassed in the contest of the lance, challenges his successful rival to wrestle: they engage, and fall together: the victory is disputed. Tucapel demands the prize for his young friend Orompello, and insults the General Caupolican. The latter is restrained from avenging the insult, by the sage advice of the veteran Colocolo, at whose request he distributes prizes of equal value to each of the claimants. To prevent farther animosities, they relinquish the rest of the appointed games, and enter into debate on the war. Lautaro is again appointed to the command of a chosen troop, and marches towards the city of Santiago. The Spaniards, alarmed at the report of his approach, send out some forces to reconnoitre his party: a skirmish ensues: they are driven back to the city, and relate that Lautaro is fortifying a strong post at some distance, intending soon to attack the city. Villagran, the Spaniard who commanded there, being confined by illness, appoints an officer of his own name to sally forth, with all the forces he can raise, in quest of the enemy.

enemy. The Spaniards fix their camp, on the approach of night, near the fort of Lautaro: they are suddenly alarmed, and summoned to arms; but the alarm is occasioned only by a single horse without a rider, which Lautaro, aware of their approach, had turned loose towards their camp, as an insulting mode of proclaiming his late victory, in which he had taken ten of the Spanish horses.

The Spaniards pass the night under arms, resolving to attack the Indians at break of day. Lautaro had issued orders that no Indian should sally from the fort under pain of death, to prevent the advantage which the Spanish cavalry must have over his small forces in the open plain. He also commanded his soldiers to retreat with an appearance of dismay, at the first attack on the fort, and suffer a considerable number of the enemy to enter the place. This stratagem succeeds: the Spaniards rush forward with great fury: the Indians give ground, but, soon turning with redoubled violence on those who had passed their lines, destroy many, and oblige the rest to save themselves by a precipitate flight. The Indians, forgetting the orders of their Leader, in the ardour of vengeance sally forth in pursuit of their flying enemy. Lautaro recalls them by the sound of a military horn, which he blows with the utmost violence. They
return,

return, but dare not appear in the prefence of their offended Commander. He iffues new reftrictions; and then, fummoning his foldiers together, addreffes them, in a fpirited, yet calm and affectionate harangue, on the neceffity of martial obedience. While he is yet fpeaking, the Spaniards return to the attack, but are again repulfed with great lofs. They retreat, and encamp at the foot of a mountain, unmolefted by any purfuers.

CANTO XII.

THE Spaniards remain in their camp, while two of their adventurous foldiers engage to return once more to the fort, and examine the ftate of it. On their approach, one of them, called Marcos Vaez, is faluted by his name, and promifed fecurity, by a voice from within the walls. Lautaro had formerly lived with him on terms of friendfhip, and now invites him into the fort. The Indian Chief harangues on the refolution and the power of his countrymen to exterminate the Spaniards, unlefs they fubmit. He propofes, however, terms of accommodation to his old friend Marcos, and fpecifies the tribute he fhould expect. The Spaniard anfwers with difdain, that the only tribute the Indians would receive from his countrymen would be
torture

torture and death. Lautaro replies, with great temper, that arms, and the valour of the respective nations, must determine this point; and proceeds to entertain his guest with a display of six Indians, whom he had mounted and trained to exercise on Spanish horses. The Spaniard challenges the whole party: Lautaro will not allow him to engage in any conflict, but dismisses him in peace. He recalls him, before he had proceeded far from the fort, and, telling him that his soldiers were much distressed by the want of provision, entreats him to send a supply, affirming it to be true heroism to relieve an enemy from the necessities of famine. The Spaniard subscribes to the sentiment, and engages, if possible, to comply with the request. Returning to his camp, he acquaints his Commander Villagran with all that had passed; who, suspecting some dangerous design from Lautaro, decamps hastily in the night to regain the city. The Indian Chief is severely mortified by their departure, as he had formed a project for cutting off their retreat, by letting large currents of water into the marshy ground on which the Spaniards were encamped. Despairing of being able to succeed against their city, now prepared to resist him, he returns towards Arauco, most sorely galled by his disappointment, and thus venting his anguish:

What can redeem Lautaro's wounded name?
What plea preserve his failing arms from shame?
Did not my ardent soul this task demand,
Which now upbraids my unperforming hand?
On me, on me alone can censure fall;
Myself th' adviser and the guide of all.
Am I the Chief who, in Fame's bright career,
Ask'd to subdue the globe a single year?

While, at the head of this my glittering train,
I weakly threaten Spanish walls in vain,
Thrice has pale Cynthia, with replenish'd ray,
Seen my ill-order'd troop in loose array;
And the rich chariot of the blazing sun
Has from the Scorpion to Aquarius run.
At last, as fugitives these paths we tread,
And mourn twice fifty brave companions dead.
Could Fate's kind hand this hateful stain efface,
Could death redeem me from this worse disgrace,
My useless spear should pierce this abject heart,
Which has so ill sustain'd a soldier's part.
Unworthy thought! the mean, ignoble blow
Would only tempt my proud and vaunting foe
To boast that I preferr'd, in fear's alarm,
My own weak weapon to his stronger arm.

By Hell I swear, who rules the sanguine strife,
If Chance allow me yet a year of life,

I'll

THIRD EPISTLE.

I'll chafe thefe foreign lords from Chile's ftrand,
And Spanifh blood fhall faturate our land.
No changing feafon, neither cold nor heat,
Shall make the firmer ftep of War retreat;
Nor fhall the earth, nor hell's expanding cave,
From this avenging arm one Spaniard fave.

Now the brave Chief, with folemn ardour, fwore
To his dear native home to turn no more;
From no fierce fun, no ftormy winds to fly,
But patiently abide the varying fky,
And fpurn all thoughts of pleafure and of eafe,
Till refcu'd fame his tortur'd foul appeafe;
Till earth confefs the brave Lautaro's hand
Has clos'd the glorious work his fpirit plann'd.
In thefe refolves the Hero found relief,
And thus relax'd the o'erftrain'd cord of grief;
Whofe preffure gall'd him with fuch mental pain,
That frenzy almoft feiz'd his burning brain.

Lautaro continues his march into an Indian diftrict, from which he collects a fmall increafe of force; and, after addreffing his foldiers concerning the expediency of ftrict military difcipline, and the caufe of their late ill fuccefs, he turns again towards the city of St. Jago; but, receiving intelligence on his road of its preparations for defence, he again fufpends his defign, and fortifies a poft, which he chufes with the hope of collecting still greater numbers to assist him in his projected enterprize. The Spaniards at St. Jago are eager to sally in quest of Lautaro, but their commander Villagran was absent on an expedition to the city of Imperial. In returning from thence he passes near the post of Lautaro. An Indian ally acquaints him with its situation, and, at the earnest request of the Spanish officer, agrees to conduct him, by a short though difficult road, over a mountain, to attack the fort by surprize. The Poet suspends his narration of this interesting event, to relate the arrival of new forces from Spain in America; and he now begins to appear himself on the field of action. " Hitherto," says he, " I have described the scenes in which I was not present; yet I have collected my information from no partial witnesses, and I have recorded only those events in which both parties agree. Since it is known that I have shed so much blood in support of what I affirm, my future narration will be more authentic; for I now speak as an ocular witness of every action, unblinded by partiality, which I disdain, and resolved to rob no one of the praise which he deserves."

After pleading his youth as an apology for the defects of his style, and after declaring that his only motive for writing was the ardent desire to preserve

THIRD EPISTLE.

so many valiant actions from perishing in oblivion, the Poet proceeds to relate the arrival of the Marquis de Canete as Viceroy in Peru, and the spirited manner in which he corrected the abuses of that country. The canto concludes with reflections on the advantages of loyalty, and the miseries of rebellion.

CANTO XIII.

SPANISH deputies from the province of Chile implore assistance from the new Viceroy of Peru: he sends them a considerable succour, under the conduct of Don Garcia, his son. The Poet is himself of this band, and relates the splendid preparations for the enterprize, and the embarkation of the troops in ten vessels, which sail from Lima towards the coast of Chile. Having described part of this voyage, he returns to the bold exploit of Villagran, and the adventures of Lautaro, the most interesting of all the Araucanian Heroes, whom he left securing himself in his sequestered fort.

A path where watchful centinels were spread,
A single path, to this lone station led:
No other signs of human step were trac'd;
For the vex'd land was desolate and waste.

It chanc'd that night the noble Chieftain preſt
His anxious miſtreſs to his gallant breaſt,
The fair Guacolda, for whoſe charms he burn'd,
And whoſe warm heart his faithful love return'd.
That night beheld the warlike ſavage reſt,
Free from th' incumbrance of his martial veſt;
That night alone allow'd his eyes to cloſe
In the deceitful calm of ſhort repoſe:
Sleep preſt upon him like the weight of death;
But ſoon he ſtarts, alarm'd, and gaſps for breath.
The fair Guacolda, with a trembling tongue,
Anxious enquires from whence his anguiſh ſprung.

 My lovely Fair! the brave Lautaro cries,
An hideous viſion ſtruck my ſcornful eyes:
Methought that inſtant a fierce Chief of Spain
Mock'd my vain ſpear with inſolent diſdain;
His forceful arm my failing powers o'ercame,
And ſtrength and motion ſeem'd to quit my frame,
But ſtill the vigour of my ſoul I keep,
And its keen anger burſt the bonds of ſleep.

 With quick deſpair, the troubled Fair one ſaid,
Alas! thy dreams confirm the ills I dread.
'Tis come—the object of my boding fears!
Thy end, the ſource of my unceaſing tears.
Yet not ſo wretched is this mournful hour,
Nor o'er me, Fortune, canſt thou boaſt ſuch pow'r,

But

But that kind death may shorten all my woes,
And give the agonizing scene to close.
Let my stern fate its cruel rage employ,
And hurl me from the throne of love and joy;
Whatever pangs its malice may devise,
It cannot rend affection's stronger ties.
Tho' horrible the blow my fears foresee,
A second blow will set my spirit free;
For cold on earth thy frame shall ne'er be found,
While mine with useless being loads the ground.

 The Chief, transported with her tender charms,
Closely around her neck entwin'd his arms;
And, while fond tears her snowy breast bedew'd,
Thus with redoubled love his speech pursu'd:

 My generous Fair, thy gloomy thoughts dismiss;
Nor let dark omens interrupt our bliss,
And cloud these moments that with transport shine,
While my exulting heart thus feels thee mine.
Thy troubled fancy prompts my mutual sigh;
Not that I think the hour of danger nigh:
But Love so melts me with his soft controul,
Impossibilities alarm my soul.
If thy kind wishes bid Lautaro live,
Who to this frame the wound of death can give?
Tho' 'gainst me all the powers of earth combine,
My life is subject to no hand but thine.

Who has reftor'd the Araucanian name,
And rais'd it, finking in the depths of fhame,
When alien lords our nation's fpirit broke,
And bent its neck beneath a fervile yoke?
I am the Chief who burft our galling chain,
And freed my country from oppreffive Spain;
My name alone, without my fword's difplay,
Humbles our foes, and fills them with difmay.
Thefe happy arms while thy dear beauties fill,
I feel no terror, I forefee no ill.
Be not by falfe and empty dreams depreft,
Since truth has nothing to afflict thy breaft.
Oft have I 'fcap'd, inur'd to every ftate,
From many a darker precipice of fate;
Oft in far mightier perils rifk'd my life,
And iffued glorious from the doubtful ftrife.

 With lefs'ning confidence, and deeper grief,
Trembling fhe hung upon the foothing Chief,
His lip with fupplicating foftnefs preft,
And urg'd with many a tear this fond requeft:

 If the pure love, which, prodigal and free,
When freedom moft was mine, I gave to thee;
If truth, which Heaven will witnefs and defend,
Weigh with my fovereign lord and gentle friend;
By thefe let me adjure thee; by the pain
Which at our parting pierc'd my every vein,

And

And all the vows, if undifpers'd in air,
Which then with many a tear I heard thee fwear;
To this my only wifh at leaft agree,
If all thy wifhes have been laws to me:
Hafte, I entreat thee, arm thyfelf with care,
And bid thy foldiers for defence prepare.

 The brave Barbarian quick reply'd—'Tis clear
How low my powers are rated by thy fear.
Canft thou fo poorly of Lautaro deem?
And is this arm fo funk in thy efteem?
This arm, which, refcuing thy native earth,
So prodigally prov'd its valiant worth!
In my try'd courage how complete thy truft,
Whofe terror weeps thy living lord as duft!

 In thee, fhe cries, with confidence moft pure,
My foul is fatisfy'd, yet not fecure.
What will thy arm avail in danger's courfe,
If my malignant fate has mightier force?
But let the mis'ry I forebode arife;
On this firm thought my conftant love relies:
The fword whofe ftroke our union may disjoin,
Will teach my faithful foul to follow thine.
Since my hard deftiny, with rage fevere,
Thus threatens me with all that love can fear;
Since I am doom'd the worft of ills to fee,
And lofe all earthly good in lofing thee;
        O! fuffer

O! suffer me to pass, ere death appears,
The little remnant of my life in tears!
The heart that sinks not in distress like this,
Could never feel, could never merit bliss.
— Here from her eyes such floods of sorrow flow,
Compassion weeps in gazing on her woe!
The fond Lautaro, tho' of firmest power,
Sheds, as she speaks, a sympathetic shower.
But, to the tender scenes of love unus'd,
My artless pen, embarrass'd and confus'd,
From its sad task with diffidence withdraws,
And in its labour asks a little pause.

CANTO XIV.

WHAT erring wretch, to Truth and Beauty blind,
Shall dare to satirize the Female Kind,
Since pure affection prompts their anxious care,
Their lovely weakness, and their fond despair?
This fair Barbarian, free from Christian ties,
A noble proof of perfect love supplies,
By kindest words, and floods of tears that roll
From the clear source of her impassion'd soul.
The cheering ardour of the dauntless Chief
Fails to afford her troubled mind relief;
Nor can the ample trench and guarded wall
Preserve her doubtful heart from fear's enthrall:

Her

Her terrors, rushing with love's mighty force,
Level whatever would impede their course.
She finds no shelter from her cruel doom,
Save the dear refuge of Lautaro's tomb.

Thus their two hearts, where equal passion reign'd,
A fond debate with tender strife maintain'd;
Their differing words alike their love display,
Feed the sweet poison, and augment its sway.

The sleepy soldiers now their stories close,
And stretch'd around their sinking fires repose.
The path in front with centinels was lin'd,
And the high mountain was their guard behind;
But o'er that mountain, with advent'rous tread,
Bold Villagran his silent forces led.
His hasty march with painful toil he made;
Toil is the price that must for fame be paid.
Now near the fort, and halting in its sight,
He waits the coming aid of clearer light.
The stars yet shining, but their fires decay,
And now the reddening East proclaims the day.
Th' advancing troop no Indian eye alarms,
For friendly darkness hover'd o'er their arms;
And on the quarter where the mountain rose,
The careless guard despis'd the thought of foes.
No panting horse their still approach betray'd;
Propitious Fortune lent the Spaniards aid;

       Fortune,

Fortune, who oft bids drowsy Sloth beware,
And lulls to sleep the watchful eye of Care.

 When Night's obscure dominion first declines,
And glimmering light the dusky air refines,
The weary guards, who round the wall were plac'd,
Hail the new day, and from their station haste;
Secure of ill, no longer watch they keep,
Quick to forget their nightly toils in sleep:
Thro' all the fort there reign'd a calm profound;
In wine and slumber all its force was drown'd.

 The Spanish Chief, who saw the fav'ring hour,
Led on by slow degrees his silent power.
No Indian eyes perceiv'd his near advance;
Fate seem'd to bind them in a cruel trance;
Each in sound slumber draws his easy breath,
Nor feels his slumber will be clos'd by Death.
So blind are mortals to that tyrant's sway,
They deem him distant, while they sink his prey.

 Our eager soldiers now no longer halt,
While kind occasion prompts the keen assault;
A shout they raise, terrific, loud, and long,
Swell'd by the voice of all the ardent throng;
Whose ranks, obedient to their Leader's call,
Rush with light ardour o'er th' unguarded wall,
And gain the fort, where Sleep's oppressive weight
Expos'd his wretched victims, blind to fate.

As

THIRD EPISTLE.

As villains, confcious of their life impure,
Find in their guilty courfe no fpot fecure;
For vice is ever doom'd new fears to feel,
And tremble at each turn of Fortune's wheel;
At every noife, at each alarm that ftirs,
Death's penal horror to their mind occurs;
Quick to their arms they fly with wild difmay,
And rufh where hafty terror points the way:
So quick the Indians to the tumult came,
With fleep and valour ftruggling in their frame.
Unaw'd by danger's unexpected fight,
They roufe their fellows, and they rufh to fight.
Tho' their brave bofoms are of armour bare,
Their manly hearts their martial rage declare.
No furious odds their gallant fouls appal,
But refolute they fly to guard the wall.

It was the feafon when, with tender care,
Lautaro reafon'd with his anxious Fair;
Careft, confol'd, and, in his anger kind,
Mildly reprov'd her weak, miftrufting mind.
Spite of his cheering voice fhe trembles ftill;
Severer terrors now her bofom fill:
For fterner founds their foft debate o'ercome,
Drown'd in the rattle of th' alarming drum.
But not fo quick, on Apprehenfion's wings,
The wretched mifer from his pillow fprings,

Whofe

Whose hoarded gold forbids his mind to rest,
If doubtful noise the nightly thief suggest:
Nor yet so hasty, tho' with terror wild,
Flies the fond mother to her wounded child,
Whose painful cry her shuddering soul alarms,
As flew Lautaro at the sound of arms.
His mantle rapidly around him roll'd,
And, grasping a light sword with hasty hold,
Too eager for his heavier arms to wait,
The fierce Barbarian hurried to the gate.
O faithless Fortune! thou deceitful friend!
Of thy false favours how severe the end!
How quick thou cancell'st, when thy frown appears,
Th' accumulated gifts of long triumphant years!

   To aid the Spaniards in their bold emprize,
Four hundred Indians march'd, their firm allies,
Who on the left their line of battle close,
And haste to combat with their painted bows;
Launching adroitly, in their rapid course,
Unnumber'd arrows with unerring force.
As brave Lautaro issued from his tent,
A shaft to meet the sallying Chief was sent;
Thro' his left side (ye valiant, mourn his lot!)
Flew the keen arrow, with such fury shot
It pierc'd his heart, the bravest and the best
That e'er was lodg'd within a human breast.

†   Proud

THIRD EPISTLE.

Proud of the stroke that laid such valour low,
Death seem'd to glory in th' important blow;
And, that no Mortal might his triumph claim,
In darkness hid the doubtful Archer's name.
Such force the keen resistless weapon found,
It stretch'd the mighty Chieftain on the ground,
And gave large outlet to his ardent blood,
That gush'd apace in a tumultuous flood.
From his sunk cheek its native colour fled;
His sightless eyes roll'd in his ghastly head;
His soul, that felt its glorious hopes o'erthrown,
Retir'd, indignant, to the world unknown.

    The noble savages, not dismayed by the death of their Leader, continue to defend the fort with great fury.

CANTO XV.

THE Poet opens this canto with a lively panegyric on Love: he affirms that the greatest Poets have derived their glory from their vivid descriptions of this enchanting passion; and he laments that he is precluded by his subject from indulging his imagination in such scenes as are more likely to captivate a reader.

    He seems to intend this as an apology (but I must

muſt own it is an unſatisfactory one) for deſerting the fair Guacolda, whom he mentions no more. He proceeds to deſcribe the ſharp conteſt which the undaunted Indians ſtill maintained in their fort:—they refuſe quarter, which is offered them by the Spaniſh Leader, and all reſolutely periſh with the brave and beloved Lautaro. The Poet then reſumes his account of the naval expedition from Peru to Chile; and concludes the canto with a ſpirited deſcription of a ſtorm, which attacked the veſſels as they arrived in ſight of the province to which they were ſteering.

CANTO XVI.

THE ſtorm abates. The Spaniards land, and fortify themſelves on an iſland near the country of the Araucanians. The latter hold a council of war in the valley of Ongolmo. Caupolican, their General, propoſes to attack the Spaniards in their new poſt. The elder Chieftains diſſuade him from the deſign. A quarrel enſues between Tucapel and the aged Peteguelen:—they are appeaſed by a ſpeech of the venerable Colocolo; by whoſe advice a ſpirited and adroit young Indian, named Millalanco, is diſpatched, as a peaceful ambaſſador, to learn the ſituation and deſigns of the Spaniards.

He

THIRD EPISTLE.

He embarks in a large galley with oars, and soon arrives at the island. He surveys the Spanish implements of war with astonishment, and is conducted to the tent of the General, Don Garcia.

CANTO XVII.

THE Indian addresses the Spanish officers with a proposal of peace and amity. He is dismissed with presents. The Chieftains, on his return, pretend to relinquish hostilities; but prepare secretly for war. The Spaniards remain unmolested on the island during the stormy season. They send a select party of an hundred and thirty, including our Poet, to raise a fort on the continent: these execute their commission with infinite dispatch, and all the Spanish troops remove to this new post. The Araucanians are alarmed. An intrepid Youth, named Gracolano, proposes to the Indian General Caupolican, to storm the fort. The Indians advance near it, under shelter of the night. The Poet describes himself, at this juncture, as oppressed by the excessive labours of the day, and unable to pursue his poetical studies according to his nightly custom: the pen falls from his hand: he is seized with violent pains and tremblings:

his strength and senses forsake him. But soon recovering from this infirmity, he enjoys a refreshing sleep. Bellona appears to him in a vision, and encourages him, both as a soldier and a poet. She conducts him through a delicious country, to the summit of a lofty mountain; when, pointing to a spot below, she informs him it is St. Quintin, and that his countrymen, under the command of their sovereign Philip, are just marching to attack it: she adds, that her presence is necessary in the midst of that important scene: and leaves the Poet on the eminence to survey and record the battle.

CANTO XVIII.

AFTER the Poet has described the success of his royal master at St. Quintin, a female figure of a most venerable appearance, but without a name, relates to him prophetically many future events of great importance to his country. She touches on the disturbances in the Netherlands, the enterprizes of the Turks, and the exploits of Don John of Austria, at that time unknown to fame. These she hints very imperfectly, telling the Poet, that if he wishes for farther information, he must follow the steps of a tame Deer, which he will find in a particular spot; this animal will lead him

him to the cell of an ancient hermit, formerly a
soldier, who will conduct him to the secret cave of
the unsocial Fiton, a mighty magician, who will
display to him the most miraculous visions. His
female Instructor then advises him to mix softer
subjects with the horrors of war, and to turn his
eyes and his thoughts to the charms of the many
Beauties who then flourished in Spain. He beholds
all these lovely fair ones assembled in a delicious
paradise: and he is particularly attracted by a
young lady, whose name he discovers to be Donna
Maria Bazan (his future wife): in the moment
that he begins to question his Guide concerning
this engaging Beauty, he is roused from his vision
by the sound of an alarm. He snatches up his arms,
and hurries to his post:—while the morning dawns,
and the Indians begin to attack the fort.

CANTO XIX.

THE Indians advance in three squadrons. The
Youth Gracolano o'erleaps the trench, supported on a lofty pike, by which he also passes the
wall. He defends himself in the midst of the Spaniards with great spirit; but, finding himself un-
supported, he wrenches a lance from a Spanish soldier, and tries to leap once more over the trench;

but he is struck by a stone while vaulting through the air, and falls, covered, as the Poet expresly declares, with two-and-thirty wounds. Some of his friends are shot near him; but the Indians get possession of the Spanish lance with which he had sprung over the wall, and brandish it in triumph. The Spaniard, named Elvira, who had lost his weapon, piqued by the adventure, sallies from the fort, and returns, amid the shouts of his countrymen, with an Indian spear which he won in single combat from a Barbarian, whom he had perceived detatched from his party. The Indians attempt to storm the fort on every side: many are destroyed by the Spanish fire-arms. The head of the ancient Peteguelen is shot off; but Tucapel passes the wall, and rushes with great slaughter into the midst of the enemy. The Spaniards who were in the ships that anchored near the coast hasten on shore, and march to assist their countrymen in the fort, but are attacked by a party of Indians in their march. The conflict continues furious on the walls; but the Indians at length retreat, leaving Tucapel still fighting within the fort.

CANTO

CANTO XX.

TUCAPEL, though severely wounded, escapes with life, and rejoins the Indian army, which continues to retreat. The Spaniards sally from the fort, but soon return to it, from the apprehension of an ambuscade. They clear their trench, and strengthen the weaker parts of their fortification. Night comes on. The Poet describes himself stationed on a little eminence in the plain below the fort, which was seated on high and rocky ground: —fatigued with the toils of the day, and oppressed by the weight of his armour, which he continues to wear, he is troubled with a lethargic heaviness: which he counteracts by exercise, declaring that his disposition to slumber in his post arose not from any intemperance either in diet or in wine, as mouldy biscuit and rain-water had been for some time his chief sustenance: and that he was accustomed to make the moist earth his bed, and to divide his time between his poetical and his military labours. He then relates the following nocturnal adventure, which may perhaps be considered as the most striking and pathetic incident in this singular poem:

While thus I strove my nightly watch to keep,
And struggled with th' oppressive weight of sleep,
As my quick feet, with many a silent stride,
Travers'd th' allotted ground from side to side,
My eye perceiv'd one quarter of the plain
White with the mingled bodies of the slain;
For our incessant fire, that bloody day,
Had slaughter'd numbers in the stubborn fray,

As oft I paus'd each distant noise to hear,
Gazing around me with attentive ear,
I heard from time to time a feeble sound
Towards the breathless Indians on the ground,
Still closing with a sigh of mournful length;
At every interval it gather'd strength;
And now it ceas'd, and now again begun,
And still from corse to corse it seem'd to run.
As night's encreasing shade my hope destroys,
To view the source of this uncertain noise,
Eager my mind's unquiet doubts to still,
And more the duties of my post fulfil,
With crouching steps I haste, and earnest eyes,
To the low spot from whence the murmurs rise;
And see a dusky Form, that seems to tread
Slow, on four feet, among the gory dead.

With terror, that my heart will not deny,
When this strange vision struck my doubtful eye,

Towards

THIRD EPISTLE.

Towards it, with a prayer to Heav'n, I prest,
Arms in my hand, my corselet on my breast;
But now the dusky Form, on which I sprung,
Upright arose, and spoke with plaintive tongue:

   Mercy! to mercy hear my just pretence;
I am a woman, guiltless of offence!
If my distress, and unexampled plight,
No generous pity in thy breast excite;
If thy blood-thirsty rage, by tears uncheck'd,
Would pass those limits which the brave respect;
Will such a deed encrease thy martial fame,
When Heaven's just voice shall to the world proclaim
That by thy ruthless sword a woman died,
A widow, sunk in sorrow's deepest tide?
Yet I implore thee, if 'twas haply thine,
Or for thy curse, as now I feel it mine;
If e'er thy lot, in any state, to prove
How firm the faithful ties of tender love,
O let me bury one brave warrior slain,
Whose corse lies blended with this breathless train!
Remember, he who thwarts the duteous will
Becomes th' approver and the cause of ill.

   Thou wilt not hinder these my pious vows;
War fiercest war, this just demand allows:
The basest tyranny alone is driven
To use the utmost power that chance has given.

Let but my foul its dear companion find,
Then fate thy fury, if to blood inclin'd;
For in fuch grief I draw my lingering breath,
Life is my dread, beyond the pangs of death.
There is no ill that now can wound my breaft,
No good, but what I in my Love poffeft:
Fly then, ye hours! that keep me from the dead;
For he, the fpirit of my life, is fled.
If adverfe Heaven my lateft wifh deny,
On his dear corfe to fix my clofing eye,
My tortur'd foul, in cruel Fate's defpight,
Will foar, the faithful partner of his flight.

 And now her agony of heart implor'd
An end of all her forrows from my fword.
Doubt and diftruft my troubled mind affail,
That fears deceit in her affecting tale;
Nor was I fully of her faith fecure,
Till oft her words the mournful truth infure;
Sufpicion whifper'd, that an artful fpy
By this illufion might our ftate defcry.

 Howe'er inclin'd to doubt, yet foon I knew,
Though night conceal'd her features from my view,
That truth was ftamp'd on every word fhe faid;
So full of grief, fo free from guilty dread:
And that bold love, to every danger blind,
Had fent her forth her flaughter'd Lord to find,
          Who,

THIRD EPISTLE.

Who, in the onset of our bloody strife,
For brave distinction sacrific'd his life.

Fill'd with compassion, when I saw her bent
To execute her chaste and fond intent,
I led her weeping to the higher spot,
To guard whose precincts was that night my lot;
Securely there I begg'd her to relate
The perfect story of her various fate;
From first to last her touching woes impart,
And by the tale relieve her loaded heart.

Ah! she replied, relief I ne'er can know,
Till Death's kind aid shall terminate my woe!
Earth for my ills no remedy supplies,
Beyond all suff'rance my afflictions rise:
Yet, though the task will agonize my soul,
Of my sad story I will tell the whole;
Grief, thus inforc'd, my life's weak thread may rend,
And in the killing tale my pangs may end.

The fair Indian then relates to Ercilla the particulars of her life, in a speech of considerable length:—she informs him, that her name is Tegualda;—that she is the daughter of the Chieftain Brancól;—that her father had often pressed her to marry, which she had for some time declined, though solicited by many of the noblest Youths in her country; till, being appointed, in compliment to her beauty, to diftribute the prizes, in a fcene of public feftivity, to thofe who excelled in the manly exercifes, fhe was ftruck by the accomplifhments of a gallant Youth, named Crepino, as fhe beftowed on him the reward of his victories; —that fhe declared her choice to her father, after perceiving the Youth infpired with a mutual affection for her;—that the old Chieftain was delighted by her chufing fo noble a character, and their marriage had been publicly folemnized but a month from that day. On this conclufion of her ftory, fhe burfts into new agonies of grief, and entreats Ercilla to let her pay her laft duties to her hufband; or rather, to unite them again in a common grave. Ercilla endeavours to confole her, by repeated promifes of all the affiftance in his power. In the moft paffionate excefs of forrow, fhe ftill entreats him to end her miferable life.—In this diftreffing fcene, our Author is relieved by the arrival of a brother officer, who had been alfo ftationed on the plain, and now informs Ercilla that the time of the appointed watch is expired. They join in comforting the unhappy Mourner, and conduct her into the fort; where they confign her, for the remainder of the night, to *the decent care of married*

married women, to use the chaste expression of the generous and compassionate Ercilla.

CANTO XXI.

IN pure affection who has soar'd above
   The tender pious proof of faithful love,
Which thus awak'd our sympathetic care
For this unhappy, fond, barbarian Fair?
O that just Fame my humble voice would raise
To swell in loudest notes her lasting praise!
To spread her merits, in immortal rhyme,
Through every language, and through every clime!

   With pitying females she the night remain'd,
Where no rude step their privacy profan'd;
Though wretched, thankful for their soothing aid,
With hopes her duty would at length be paid.

   Soon as the welcome light of morning came,
Though soundest sleep had seiz'd my jaded frame,
Though my tir'd limbs were still to rest inclin'd,
Solicitude awak'd my anxious mind.
Quick to my Indian Mourner I repair,
And still in tears I find the restless Fair;
The varying hours afford her no relief,
No transient momentary pause of grief.

                              With

With trueft pity I her pangs affuage;
To find her flaughter'd Lord my word engage,
Reftore his corfe, and, with a martial band,
Efcort her fafely to her native land.
With blended doubt and forrow, weeping ftill,
My promis'd word fhe pray'd me to fulfil.

Affembling now a menial Indian train,
I led her to explore the bloody plain:
Where heaps of mingled dead deform'd the ground,
Near to the fort the breathlefs Chief we found;
Clay-cold and ftiff, the gory earth he preft,
A fatal ball had pafs'd his manly breaft.

Wretched Tegualda, who before her view'd
The pale disfigur'd form, in blood imbru'd,
Sprung forward, and with inftantaneous force
Frantic fhe darted on the precious corfe,
And prefs'd his lips, where livid death appears,
And bath'd his wounded bofom in her tears,
And kifs'd the wound, and the wild hope purfues
That her fond breath may yet new life infufe.

Wretch that I am! at length fhe madly cried,
Why does my foul thefe agonies abide?
Why do I linger in this mortal ftrife,
Nor pay to Love his juft demand, my life?
Why, poor of fpirit! at a fingle blow
Do I not clofe this bitter fcene of woe?

Whence

THIRD EPISTLE.

Whence this delay? will Heaven to me deny
The wretch's choice and privilege, to die?
    While, bent on death, in this despair she gasp'd,
Her furious hands her snowy neck inclasp'd;
Failing her frantic wish, they do not spare
Her mournful visage nor her flowing hair.
Much as I strove to stop her mad intent,
Her fatal purpose I could scarce prevent:
So loath'd she life, and with such fierce controul
The raging thirst of death inflam'd her soul.
    When by my prayers, and soft persuasion's balm,
Her pangs of sorrow grew a little calm,
And her mild speech confirm'd my hope, at last,
That her delirious agony was past,
My ready Indian train, with duteous haste,
On a firm-bier the clay-cold body plac'd,
And bore the Warrior, in whose fate we griev'd,
To where her vassals the dear charge receiv'd.
But, lest from ruthless War's outrageous sway
The mourning Fair might suffer on her way,
O'er the near mountains, to a safer land,
I march'd to guard her with my warlike band;
And there secure, for the remaining road
Was clear and open to her own abode,
She gratefully declin'd my farther care,
And thank'd and bless'd me in a parting prayer.

As I have been tempted to dwell much longer than I intended on some of the most pathetic incidents of this extraordinary poem, I shall give a more concise summary of the remaining cantos. ——On Ercilla's return, the Spaniards continue to strengthen their fort. They receive intelligence from an Indian ally, that the Barbarian army intend a fresh assault in the night. They are relieved from this alarm by the arrival of a large reinforcement from the Spanish cities in Chile:—on which event Colocolo prevails on the Indians to suspend the attack. Caupolican, the Indian General, reviews all his forces; and the various Chieftains are well described. The Spanish Commander, Don Garcia, being now determined to march into the hostile district of Arauco, addresses his soldiers in a spirited harangue, requesting them to remember the pious cause for which they fight, and to spare the life of every Indian who is disposed to submission. They remove from their post, and pass in boats over the broad river Biobio.

CANTO XXII.

THE Spaniards are attacked in their new quarters—a furious battle ensues. The Spaniards are forced to give ground, but at last prevail. The Indian

Indian Chief, Rengo, fignalizes himfelf in the action; defends himfelf in a marfh, and retreats in good order with his forces. The Spaniards, after the conflict, feize an unhappy ftraggling Youth, named Galvarino, whom they punifh as a rebel in the moft barbarous manner, by cutting off both his hands. The valiant Youth defies their cruelty in the midft of this horrid fcene; and, brandifhing his bloody ftumps, departs from his oppreffors with the moft infulting menaces of revenge.

CANTO XXIII.

GALVARINO appears in the Affembly of the Indian Chieftains, and excites them, in a very animated fpeech, to revenge the barbarity with which he had been treated. He faints from lofs of blood, in the clofe of his harangue, but is recovered by the care of his friends, and reftored to health. The Indians, exafperated by the fight of his wounds, unanimoufly determine to profecute the war. The Spaniards, advancing in Arauco, fend forth fcouts to difcover the difpofition of the neighbouring tribes. Ercilla, engaging in this fervice, perceives an old Indian in a fequeftered fpot, apparently finking under the infirmities of age;

age; but, on his approach, the ancient figure flies from him with aftonifhing rapidity. He endeavours in vain, though on horfeback, to overtake this aged fugitive, who foon efcapes from his fight. He now difcovers the tame Deer foretold in his vifion; and, purfuing it, is conducted through intricate paths to a retired cottage, where a courteous old man receives him in a friendly manner. Ercilla enquires after the magician Fiton: the old man undertakes to guide him to the fecret manfion of that wonderful Necromancer, to whom he declares himfelf related. He adds, that he himfelf was once a diftinguifhed warrior; but, having the misfortune to fully his paft glory, without lofing his life, in a conflict with another Chieftain, he had withdrawn himfelf from fociety, and lived twenty years as a hermit. He now leads Ercilla through a gloomy grove to the cell of the Magician, whofe refidence and magical apparatus are defcribed with great force of imagination. Fiton appears from a fecret portal, and proves to be the aged figure who had efcaped fo fwiftly from the fight of Ercilla. At the requeft of his relation, the old Warrior, he condefcends to fhew Ercilla the wonders of his art. He leads him to à large lucid globe, felf-fufpended in the middle of an immenfe apartment. He tells him it is the work of forty years

years study, and contains an exact representation of the world, with this singular power, that it exhibits, at his command, any scene of futurity which he wishes to behold:—that, knowing the heroic composition of Ercilla, he will give him an opportunity to vary and embellish his poem by the description of a most important sea-fight, which he will display to him most distinctly on that sphere. He then invokes all the powers of the infernal world. Ercilla fixes his eye on the globe, and perceives the naval forces of Spain, with those of the Pope and the Venetians, prepared to engage the great armament of the Turks.

CANTO XXIV.

DESCRIBES circumstantially the naval battle of Lepanto, and celebrates the Spanish admiral, Don John of Austria. Ercilla gazes with great delight on this glorious action, and beholds the complete triumph of his countrymen; when the Magician strikes the globe with his wand, and turns the scene into darkness. Ercilla, after being entertained with other marvellous sights, which he omits from his dread of prolixity, takes leave of his two aged friends, and regains his quarters. The Spaniards

Spaniards continue to advance: on their pitching their camp in a new spot, towards evening, an Araucanian, fantastically drest in armour, enquires for the tent of Don Garcia, and is conducted to his presence.

CANTO XXV.

THE Araucanian delivers a defiance to Don Garcia, in the name of Caupolican, who challenges the Spanish General to end the war by a single combat. The messenger adds, that the whole Indian army will descend into the plain, on the next morning, to be spectators of the duel. Don Garcia dismisses him with an acceptance of the challenge. At the dawn of day the Indian forces appear in three divisions. A party of Spanish horse precipitately attack their left wing, before which Caupolican was advancing. They are repulsed. A general and obstinate engagement ensues. The mangled Galvarino appears at the head of one Indian squadron, and excites his countrymen to revenge his wrongs. Many Spaniards are named who distinguish themselves in the battle. Among the Indian Chiefs Tucapel and Rengo display the most splendid acts of valour; and, though

though personal enemies, they mutually defend each other. Caupolican also, at the head of the left squadron, obliges the Spaniards to retreat; and the Araucanians are on the point of gaining a decisive victory, when the fortune of the day begins to turn.

CANTO XXVI.

THE reserved guard of the Spaniards, in which Ercilla was stationed, advancing to the charge, recover the field, and oblige the main body of the Indians to fly. Caupolican, though victorious in his quarter, sounds a retreat when he perceives this event. The Indians fly in great disorder. Rengo for some time sustains an unequal conflict, and at last retreats sullenly into a wood, where he collects several of the scattered fugitives. As Ercilla happened to advance towards this spot, a Spaniard, called Remon, exhorts him by name to attempt the dangerous but important exploit of forcing this Indian party from the wood. His honour being thus piqued, he rushes forward with a few followers, and, after an obstinate engagement, in which many of the Indians are cut to pieces, the Spaniards obtain the victory, and return to their camp with several prisoners. After this great defeat of the Indian army, the Spaniards, to deter their enemies from all future refiftance, barbaroufly refolve to execute twelve Chieftains of diftinction, whom they find among their captives, and to leave their bodies expofed on the trees that furrounded the field of battle. The generous Ercilla, lamenting this inhuman fentence, intercedes particularly for the life of one, alledging that he had feen him united with the Spaniards. - This perfon proves to be Galvarino; who, on hearing the interceffion for his life, produces his mangled arms, which he had concealed in his bofom, and, giving vent to his deteftation of the Spaniards, infifts on dying with his countrymen. Ercilla perfifts in vain in his endeavour to fave him. As no executioner could be found among the Spanifh foldiers, a new mode of deftruction, fays our Poet, was invented; and every Indian was ordered to terminate his own life by a cord which was given him. Thefe brave men haftened to accomplifh their fate with as much alacrity, continues Ercilla, as the moft fpirited warrior marches to an attack. One alone of the twelve begins to hefitate, and pray for mercy; declaring himfelf the lineal defcendant of the moft ancient race and fovereign of the country. He is interrupted by the reproaches of the impetuous Galvarino, and, repenting his timidity, atones for it by inftant death.

The

The Spaniards advance still farther in the country, and raise a fort where Valdivia had perished. Ercilla finds his old friend the Magician once more, who tells him that Heaven thought proper to punish the pride of the Araucanians by their late defeat; but that the Spaniards would soon pay dearly for their present triumph. The Wizard retires after this prophesy, and, with much intreaty, allows Ercilla to follow him. Coming to a gloomy rock, he strikes it with his wand; a secret door opens, and they enter into a delicious garden, which the Poet commends for its symmetry, expressly declaring that every hedge *has its brother*. The Magician leads him into a vault of alabaster; and, perceiving his wish, though he does not express it, of seeing the miraculous globe again, the courteous Fiton conducts him to it.

CANTO XXVII.

THE Magician displays to our Poet the various countries of the globe; particularly pointing out to him the ancient castle of Ercilla, the seat of his ancestors in Biscay, and the spot where his sovereign Philip the Second was soon to build his magnificent palace, the Escurial. Having shewn him

him the various nations of the earth on his marvelˆlous fphere, Fiton conducts his gueft to the road leading to the Spanifh camp, where the foldiers of Ercilla were feeking their officer. The Spaniards in vain attempt to foothe and to terrify the Araucanians into peace; and, finding the importance of their prefent poft, they determine to ftrengthen it. Ercilla proceeds with a party to the city of Imperial, to provide neceffaries for this purpofe. On his return, as he is marching through the country of fome pacific Indians, he difcovers, at the clofe of day, a diftreft female, who attempts to fly, but is overtaken by Ercilla.

CANTO XXVIII.

THE fair fugitive, whom our Poet defcribes as fingularly beautiful, relates her ftory. She tells him her name is Glaura, the daughter of an opulent Chieftain, with whom fhe lived moft happily, till a brother of her father's, who frequently refided with him, perfecuted her with an unwarrantable paffion;—that fhe in vain reprefented to him the impious nature of his love;—he perfifted in his frantic attachment, and, on the appearance of a hoftile party of Spaniards, rufhed forth to die in her defence,

defence, intreating her to receive his departing
spirit. He fell in the action; her father shared
the same fate: she herself escaped at a postern-gate
into the woods. Two negroes, laden with spoil,
discovered, and seized her. Her cries brought a
young Indian, named Cariolano, to her rescue: he
shot an arrow into the heart of the first ruffian, and
stabbed the second. Glaura expressed her gratitude
by receiving her young deliverer as her husband.
Before they could regain a place of safety, they
were alarmed by the approach of Spaniards. The
generous Youth intreated Glaura to conceal herself in a tree, while he ventured to meet the enemy. In her terror she submitted to this expedient,
which, on recovery from her panic, she bitterly repented; for when she issued from her retreat, she
sought in vain for Cariolano, and supposed, from the
clamour she had heard, that he must have perished.
She continued to wander in this wretched state of
mind, still unable to hear any tidings of her protec-
tor. While the fair Indian thus closes her narrative, Ercilla is alarmed by the approach of a large
party of Barbarians. One of his faithful Indian
attendants, whom he had lately attached to him,
intreats him to escape with the utmost haste;
adding, that he can save him from pursuit by his
knowledge of the country; and that he will risque

his own life moft willingly, to preferve that of Ercilla. Glaura burfts into an agony of joy, in difcovering her loft Cariolano in this faithful attendant. Ercilla exclaims, " Adieu, my friends; I " give you both your liberty, which is all I have " at prefent to beftow," and rejoins his little troop. Before he enters on the account of what followed, he relates the circumftance by which he attached Cariolano to his fervice; whom he had found alone, as he himfelf was marching with a fmall party, and a few prifoners that he had taken. The Youth at firft defended himfelf, and fhot two Spaniards with his arrows, and continued to refift the numbers that preffed upon him with his mantle and his dagger, evading their blows by his extreme agility, and wounding feveral. Ercilla generoufly rufhed in to his refcue, and declared he deferved a reward for his uncommon bravery, inftead of being deftroyed fo unfairly. The Youth, in confequence of this treatment, flung down his dagger, and became the affectionate attendant of Ercilla. Our Poet, after relating this incident, returns to the fcene where his party was furprized in a hollow road, and feverely galled by the enemy, who attacked them with fhowers of ftones from the higher ground. Ercilla forces his way up the precipice, and, after difperfing part of the Indian force, effects his efcape with
a few

a few followers; but all are wounded, and obliged to leave their baggage in the poffeffion of their numerous enemies.

CANTO XXIX.

OPENS with an encomium on the love of our country, and the fignal proofs of this virtue which the Araucanians difplayed; who, notwithftanding their lofs of four great battles in the fpace of three months, ftill continue firm in their refolution of defending their liberty. Caupolican propofes, in a public affembly, to fet fire to their own habitations, and leave themfelves no alternative, but that of killing or being killed. The Chieftains all agree in this defperate determination. Tucapel, before they proceed to action againft the Spaniards, infifts on terminating his difference with Rengo, a rival Chieftain, by a fingle combat. A plain is appointed for this purpofe: all the people of Arauco affemble as fpectators: the Chiefs appear in complete armour, and engage in a moft obftinate and bloody conflict.

CANTO XXX.

AFTER many dreadful wounds on each fide, the two Chieftains, clofing with each other, fall

fall together, and, after a fruitless struggle for victory, remain speechless on the ground. Caupolican, who presided as judge of the combat, descends from his seat, and finding some signs of life in each, orders them to be carried to their respective tents. They recover, and are reconciled. The Spaniards, leaving a garrison in their new fort, under a captain named Reynoso, had proceeded to the city of Imperial. Caupolican endeavours to take advantage of this event. He employs an artful Indian, named Pran, to examine the state of the fort. Pran insinuates himself among the Indian servants belonging to the Spaniards. He views the fort, and endeavours to persuade a servile Indian, named Andresillo, to admit Caupolican and his forces while the Spaniards are sleeping. Andresillo promises to meet Caupolican in secret, and converse with him on this project.

CANTO XXXI.

OPENS with a spirited invective against treachery in war, and particularly those traitors who betray their country. Andresillo reveals all that had passed to his Spanish captain; who promises him a great reward if he will assist in making the stratagem of the Indians an instrument of destruction

tion to thofe who contrived it. They concert a plan for this purpofe. Andrefillo meets Caupolican in fecret, and promifes to introduce the Indian forces into the fort when the Spaniards are fleeping in the heat of the day. Pran is fent forward, to learn from Andrefillo if all things are quiet, juft before the hour appointed for the affault. He examines the ftate of the fort, and, finding the Spaniards apparently unprepared for defence, haftens back to the Indian General, who advances by a quick and filent march. The Spaniards in the interim point all their guns, and prepare for the moft bloody refiftance.

CANTO XXXII.

AFTER a panegyric on clemency, and a noble cenfure of thofe enormous cruelties, by which his countrymen fullied their military fame, the Poet relates the dreadful carnage which enfued as the Indians approached the fort. The Spaniards, after deftroying r mbers by their artillery, fend forth a party of horfe, who cut the fugitives to pieces. They inhumanly murder thirteen of their moft diftinguifhed prifoners, by blowing them from the mouths of cannon: but none of the confederate Chieftains, whom the Poet has particularly

larly celebrated, were included in this number; for those high-spirited Barbarians had refused to attend Caupolican in this assault, as they considered it as disgraceful to attack their enemies by surprize. The unfortunate Indian Leader, seeing his forces thus unexpectedly massacred, escapes with ten faithful followers, and wanders through the country in the most calamitous condition. The Spaniards endeavour, by all the means they can devise, to discover his retreat: the faithful inhabitants of Arauco refuse to betray him.

Ercilla, in searching the country with a small party, finds a young wounded female. She informs him, that marching with her husband, she had the misfortune of seeing him perish in the late slaughter;—that a friendly soldier, in pity to her extreme distress, had tried to end her miserable life in the midst of the confusion, but had failed in his generous design, by giving her an ineffectual wound;—that she had been removed from the field of battle to that sequestered spot, where she languished in the hourly hope of death, which she now implores from the hand of Ercilla. Our Poet consoles her; dresses her wound, and leaves one of his attendants to protect her. On his return to the fort, he discourses to his soldiers in praise of the fidelity and spirit displayed by the Indian females,

THIRD EPISTLE.

males, comparing them to the chaste and constant Dido. A young soldier of his train expresses his surprize on hearing Ercilla commend the Carthaginian Queen for a virtue to which, he conceived, she had no pretence. From hence our Poet takes occasion to vindicate the injured Eliza from the slanderous misrepresentation of Virgil; and flatters himself that the love of justice, so natural to man, will induce every reader to listen with pleasure to his defence of the calumniated Queen. He then enters on her *real history*, and relates circumstantially her lamentation over the murdered Sichæus, and the artifice by which she escaped with her treasures from her inhuman brother Pygmalion:—she engages many of his attendants to share the chances of her voyage; and, having collected a supply of females from the island of Cyprus, she directs her course to the coast of Africa.

CANTO XXXIII.

DIDO, as our Poet continues her *more authentic story*, purchases her dominion and raises her flourishing city. The ambassadors of Iarbas arrive at Carthage, to offer this celebrated Queen the alternative of marriage or war. The Senate, who are first informed of the proposal, being fearful that the

the chaste resolutions of their fair Sovereign may ruin their country, attempt to engage her, by a singular device, to accept the hand of Iarbas. They tell her, that this haughty Monarch has sent to demand twenty of her privy counsellors to regulate his kingdom; and that, in consideration of their age and infirmities, they must decline so unpleasant a service. The Queen represents to them the danger of their refusal, and the duty which they owe to their country; declaring that she would most readily sacrifice her own life for the safety or advantage of her subjects. The Senators then reveal to her the real demand of Iarbas, and urge the necessity of her marriage for the preservation of the state. The faithful Dido knows not what to resolve, and demands three months to consider of this delicate and important point:—at the close of that period, she assembles her subjects, and, taking leave of them in a very affectionate harangue, declares her resolution to die, as the only means by which she can at once satisfy both Heaven and earth, by discharging her duty to her people, and at the same time preserving her faith inviolate to her departed Sichæus. Invoking his name, she plunges a poniard in her breast; and throws herself on a flaming pile, which had been kindled for a different sacrifice. Her grateful subjects lament her death,

and

and pay divine honours to her memory. "This *
(fays our Poet) is the true and genuine ſtory of the
famous defamed Dido, whoſe moſt honoured chaſ-
tity has been belied by the inconſiderate Virgil, to
embelliſh his poetical fictions."

Our Poet returns from this digreſſion on Dido,
to the fate of the Indian Leader Caupolican.—One
of the priſoners, whom the Spaniards had taken
in their ſearch after this unfortunate Chief, is at
laſt tempted by bribes to betray his General. He
conducts the Spaniards to a ſpot near the ſequeſtered
retreat of Caupolican, and directs them how to
diſcover it; but refuſes to advance with them,
overcome by his dread of the Hero whom he is
tempted to betray. The Spaniards ſurround the
houſe in which the Chieftain had taken refuge
with his ten faithful aſſociates. Alarmed by a
ſentinel, he prepares for defence; but being

---

* Eſte es el cierto y verdadero cuento,
De la famoſa Dido disfamada
Que Virgilio Maron ſin miramiento
Falſeó ſu hiſtoria y caſtidad preciada
Por dar a ſus ficciones ornamento
Pues vemos que eſta Reyna importunada
Pudiéndoſe caſar y no quemarſe
Antes quemarſe quiſo, que caſarſe.

ſoon

soon wounded in the arm, surrenders, endeavouring to conceal his high character, and to make the Spaniards believe him an ordinary soldier.

With their accustom'd shouts, and greedy toil,
Our furious troops now riot in their spoil;
Through the lone village their quick rapine spread,
Nor leave unpillag'd e'en a single shed:
When, from a tent, that, plac'd on safer ground,
The neighbouring hill's uncultur'd summit crown'd,
A woman rush'd, who, in her hasty flight,
Ran through the roughest paths along the rocky height.
A Negro of our train, who mark'd her way,
Soon made the hapless fugitive his prey;
For thwarting crags her doubtful steps impede,
And the fair form was ill prepar'd for speed;
For at her breast she bore her huddled son;
To fifteen months the infant's life had run:
From our brave captive sprung the blooming boy,
Of both his parents the chief pride and joy.
The Negro carelessly his victim brought,
Nor knew th' important prize his haste had caught.
  Our soldiers now, to catch the cooling tide,
Had sallied to the murmuring river's side:
                                        When

THIRD EPISTLE.

When the unhappy Wife beheld her Lord,
His strong arms bound with a disgraceful cord,
Stript of each ensign of his past command,
And led the pris'ner of our shouting band;
Her anguish burst not into vain complaint,
No female terrors her firm soul attaint;
But, breathing fierce disdain, and anger wild,
Thus she exclaim'd, advancing with her child:
 The stronger arm that in this shameful band
Has tied thy weak effeminated hand,
Had nobler pity to thy state exprest
If it had bravely pierc'd that coward breast.
Wert thou the Warrior whose heroic worth
So swiftly flew around the spacious earth,
Whose name alone, unaided by thy arm,
Shook the remotest clime with fear's alarm?
Wert thou the Victor whose triumphant strain
Promis'd with rapid sword to vanquish Spain;
To make new realms Arauco's power revere,
And spread her empire o'er the Arctic sphere?
Wretch that I am! how was my heart deceiv'd,
In all the noble pride with which it heav'd,
When through the world my boasted title ran,
Tresia, the wife of great Caupolican!
Now, plung'd in misery from the heights of fame,
My glories end in this detested shame,

To see thee captive in a lonely spot,
When death and honour might have been thy lot!
  What now avail thy scenes of happier strife,
So dearly bought by many a nobler life;
The wondrous feats, that valour scarce believ'd,
By thee with hazard and with toil atchiev'd?
Where are the vaunted fruits of thy command,
The laurels gather'd by this fetter'd hand?
All sunk! all turn'd to this abhorr'd disgrace,
To live the slave of this ignoble race!
Say, had thy soul no strength, thy hand no lance,
To triumph o'er the fickle pow'r of chance?
Dost thou not know, that, to the Warrior's name,
A gallant exit gives immortal fame?
  Behold the burthen which my breast contains,
Since of thy love no other pledge remains!
Hadst thou in glory's arms resign'd thy breath,
We both had follow'd thee in joyous death:
Take, take thy Son! he was a tie most dear,
Which spotless love once made my heart revere;
Take him!—by generous pain, and wounded pride,
The currents of this fruitful breast are dried;
Rear him thyself, for thy gigantic frame,
To woman turn'd, a woman's charge may claim:
A mother's title I no more desire,
Or shameful children from a shameful sire!

As

As thus she spoke, with growing madness stung,
The tender nursling from her arms she flung
With savage fury, hast'ning from our sight,
While anguish seem'd to aid her rapid flight.
Vain were our efforts; our indignant cries,
Nor gentle prayers, nor angry threats, suffice
To make her breast, where cruel frenzy burn'd,
Receive the little innocent she spurn'd.

The Spaniards, after providing a nurse for this unfortunate child, return with their prisoner Caupolican to their fort, which they enter in triumph.

The Indian General, perceiving that all attempts to conceal his quality are ineffectual, desires a conference with the Spanish Captain Reynoso.

CANTO XXXIV.

CAUPOLICAN entreats Reynoso to grant his life, but without any signs of terror. He affirms it will be the only method of appeasing the sanguinary hatred by which the contending nations are inflamed; and he offers, from his great influence over his country, to introduce the Christian worship, and to bring the Araucanians to consider

consider themselves as the subjects of the Spanish Monarch. His proposals are rejected, and he is sentenced to be impaled, and shot to death with arrows. He is unappall'd by this decree; but first desires to be publicly baptized: after which ceremony, he is inhumanly led in chains to a scaffold. He displays a calm contempt of death; but, on seeing a wretched Negro appointed his executioner, his indignation bursts forth, and he hurls the Negro from the scaffold, entreating to die by a more honourable hand. His horrid sentence is however executed. He supports the agonies of the stake with patient intrepidity, till a chosen band of archers put a period to his life.

Our brave Ercilla expresses his abhorrence of this atrocious scene; and adds, that if he had been present, this cruel execution should not have taken place.

The consequence of it was such as Caupolican foretold:—the Araucanians determine to revenge his death, and assemble to elect a new General. The Poet makes an abrupt transition from their debate, to relate the adventures of Don Garcia, with whom he was himself marching to explore new regions. The inhabitants of the districts they invade, alarmed at the approach of the Spaniards,

niards, confult on the occafion. An Indian, named Tunconabala, who had ferved under the Araucanians, addreffes the affembly, and recommends to them a mode of eluding the fuppofed avaricious defigns of the Spaniards, by fending meffengers to them, who fhould affume an appearance of extreme poverty, and reprefent their country as barren, and thus induce the invaders to turn their arms towards a different quarter. He offers to engage in this fervice himfelf. The Indians adopt the project he recommends, and remove their valuable effects to the interior parts of their country.

CANTO XXXV.

DON GARCIA being arrived at the boundaries of Chile, which no Spaniard had paffed, encourages his foldiers, in a fpirited harangue, to the acquifition of the new provinces which lay before them. They enter a rude and rocky country, in which they are expofed to many hazards by their deceitful guides. Tunconabala meets them, as he had projected, with the appearance of extreme poverty; and, after many affurances of the fterility of that region, advifes them to return, or to advance by a different path, which he reprefents to them as dangerous, but the only practicable road. On finding

finding them resolved to press forward, he supplies them with a guide. They advance, with great toil and danger. Their guide escapes from them. They continue their march, through various hardships, in a desolate region. They at length discover a fertile plain, and a large lake with many little inhabited islands. As they approach the lake, a large gondola, with twelve oars, advances to meet them: the party it contained leap ashore, and salute the Spaniards with expressions of amity.

CANTO XXXVI.

THE young Chieftain of the gondola supplies the Spaniards with provisions, refusing to accept any reward: and our Poet celebrates all the inhabitants of this region, for their amiable simplicity of manners. He visits one of the principal islands, where he is kindly entertained. He discovers that the lake had a communication with the sea, by a very rough and dangerous channel: this circumstance obliges the Spaniards, though reluctant, to return. They lament the necessity of passing again through the hardships of their former road. A young Indian undertakes to conduct them by an easier way. But our adventurous Ercilla, before the little army set forth on their return, engages

THIRD EPISTLE.

gages ten chosen associates to embark with him in a small vessel, and pass the dangerous channel. He lands on a wild and sandy spot, and, advancing half a mile up the country, engraves a stanza, to record this adventure, on the bark of a tree. He repasses the channel, and rejoins the Spanish troops: who, after much difficulty, reach the city of Imperial. Our Poet then touches on some particulars of his personal history, which I mention in the slight sketch of his life. He afterwards promises his reader to relate the issue of the debate among the Araucanian Chieftains, on the election of their new General; but, recollecting in the instant that Spain herself is in arms, he entreats the favour of his Sovereign to inspire him with new spirit, that he may devote himself to that higher and more interesting subject.

CANTO XXXVII.

OUR Poet, in this his last canto, seems to begin a new work. He enters into a discussion of Philip's right to the dominion of Portugal, and his acquisition of that kingdom; when, sinking under the weight of this new subject, he declares his resolution of leaving it to some happier Poet. He recapitulates the various perils and hardships of his

his own life, and, remarking that he has ever been unfortunate, and that all his labours are unrewarded, he confoles himfelf with the reflection, that honour confifts not in the poffeffion of rewards, but in the confcioufnefs of having deferved them. He concludes with a pious refolution to withdraw himfelf from the vain purfuits of the world, and to devote himfelf to God.

NOTE XI. VERSE 280.

At once the Bard of Glory and of Love.] The Epic powers of Camoens have received their due honour in our language, by the elegant and fpirited

---

SONETO I.

EM quanto quis Fortuna que tiveffe
    Efperança de algum contentamento,
O gofto de hum fuave penfamento
Me fez que feus effeytos efcreveffe.
Porèm temendo Amor queavifo deffe
    Minha efcritura a algum juizo ifento,
    Efcureccome o engenho co' o tormento,
Para que feus enganos naõ diffeffe

O vós,

rited tranflation of Mr. Mickle; but our country is ftill a ftranger to the lighter graces and pathetic fweetnefs of his fhorter compofitions. Thefe, as they are illuftrated by the Spanifh notes of his indefatigable Commentator, *Manuel de Faria*, amount to two volumes in folio, I fhall prefent the reader with a fpecimen of his Sonnets, for which he is celebrated as the rival of Petrarch. Of the three tranflations which follow, I am indebted for the two firft to an ingenious friend, from whom the public may wifh me to have received more extenfive obligations of a fimilar nature. It may be proper to add, that the firft Sonnet of Camoens, like that of Petrarch, is a kind of preface to the amorous poetry of its author.

SONNET I.

While on my head kind Fortune deign'd to pour
    Her lavifh boons, and through my willing foul
Made tides of extafy and pleafure roll,
I fung the raptures of each paffing hour.
But Love, who heard me praife the golden fhower,
Refolv'd my fond prefumption to controul;
And painful darknefs o'er my fpirit ftole,
Left I fhould dare to tell his treacherous power.
                                                    O ye,

O vós, que amor obriga a ſer ſogeytos
  A diverſas vontades! quando lerdes
  Num breve livro caſos tão diverſos;
Verdades puras ſaõ, & naõ defeytos.
  Entendey que ſegundo o amor tiverdes,
  Tircis o entendimento de meus verſos.

SONETO XIX.

ALMA minha gentil, que te partiſte
  Taõ cedo deſta vida deſcontente,
  Repouſa lâ no ceo eternamente,
E viva eu cà na terra ſempre triſte.
Se là no aſſento etereo, onde ſubiſte,
  Memoria deſta vida ſe conſente,
  Naõ te eſqueças de aquelle amor ardente.
Que já nos olhos meus taõ puro viſte.
Eſe vires que póde merecerte
  Algũa couſa a dor queme ficou
  Da magoa, ſem remedio, de perderte,
Roga a Deos que teus annos encurtou,
  Que taõ cedo de cà me leve a verte,
  Quaõ cedo de meus olhos te levou.

SONETO

O ye, whom his hard yoke compels to bend
To others' will, if in my various lay
Sad plaints ye find, and fears, and cruel wrong,
To suffering nature and to truth attend;
For in the measure ye have felt his sway,
Your sympathizing hearts will feel my song.

SONNET XIX.

ON THE DEATH OF THE POET'S MISTRESS,
DONNA CATALINA DE ATAIDE,
WHO DIED AT THE AGE OF TWENTY.

GO, gentle spirit! now supremely blest,
    From scenes of pain and struggling virtue go:
From thy immortal seat of heavenly rest
Behold us lingering in a world of woe!
And if beyond the grave, to saints above,
Fond memory still the transient past pourtrays,
Blame not the ardour of my constant love,
Which in these longing eyes was wont to blaze.
But if from virtue's source my sorrows rise,
For the sad loss I never can repair,
Be thine to justify my endless sighs,
And to the Throne of Grace prefer thy prayer,
That Heaven, who made thy span of life so brief,
May shorten mine, and give my soul relief.

SONETO LXXII.

QUANDO de minhas magoas a comprida
Maginaçaõ os olhos me adormece,
Em sonhos aquella alma me aparece
Que para mi foy sonho nesta vida.
Lá numa soidade, onde estendida
A vista por o campo desfallece,
Corro apos ella; & ella entaõ parece
Que maes de mi se alonga, compelida,
Brado: Naõ me fujays, sombra benina.
Ella (os olhos em mi c'hum brado pejo,
Como quem diz, que ja naõ pode ser)
Torna a fugirme: torno a bradar; dina:
E antes q' acabe em mene, acordo, & vejo
Que nem hum breve engano posso ter.

The Spanish Commentator of Camoens considers this vision as the most exquisite Sonnet of his author, and affirms that it is superior to the much longer poem of Petrarch's, on a similar idea. It may amuse a curious reader to compare both Camoens and Petrarch, on this occasion, with Milton, who has also written a Sonnet on the same subject. The Commentator Faria has a very

pleasant

SONNET LXXII.

While preſt with woes from which it cannot flee,
  My fancy ſinks, and ſlumber ſeals my eyes;
Her ſpirit haſtens in my dreams to riſe,
Who was in life but as a dream to me.
O'er a drear waſte, ſo wide no eye can ſee
How far its ſenſe-evading limit lies,
I follow her quick ſtep; but ah! ſhe flies!
Our diſtance widening by ſtern Fate's decree.
Fly not from me, kind ſhadow! I exclaim:
She, with fix'd eyes, that her ſoft thoughts reveal,
And ſeem to ſay, "Forbear thy fond deſign!"
Still flies!—I call her; but her half-form'd name
Dies on my falt'ring tongue.—I wake, and feel
Not e'en one ſhort deluſion may be mine.

---

pleaſant remark on this ſpecies of compoſition. He vindicates the dignity of the amorous Sonnet, by producing an alphabetical liſt of two hundred great Poets, who have thus complimented the object of their affection: and he very gravely introduces Achilles as the leader of this choir, for having celebrated Briſeis. If the Sonnets of the Portugueſe Poet are worthy of attention,

his

his Elegies are perhaps still more so, as they illustrate many particulars of his interesting life, which ended in 1579, under the most cruel circumstances of neglect and poverty.

Portugal has produced no less than fourteen Epic poems; twelve in her own language, and two in that of Spain. At the head of these stands the Lusiad of Camoens. The Malaca Conquistada of Francisco de Sa' de Menesis — and the Ulyssea, or Lisboa Edificada, of Gabriel Pereira de Castro, are two of the most eminent among its successors. — For a list of the Portuguese Epic Poets, and for an elegant copy of the Malaca Conquistada, I am indebted to the very liberal politeness of the Chevalier de Pinto, the Ambassador of Portugal.

NOTE XII. VERSE 287.

Where Eulogy, with one eternal smile.] Though a vain insipidity may be considered as the general characteristic of the French *Eloges*, it is but just to remark, that several of these performances are an honour to the country which produced them; and particularly the little volume of *Eloges* lately published by Mr. D'Alembert. This agreeable Encomiast has varied and enlivened the tone

of panegyric by the moſt happy mixture of amu-
ſing anecdote, judicious criticiſm, and philoſo-
phical precept: we may juſtly ſay of him, what
he himſelf has ſaid of his predeceſſor Fontenelle:
Il a ſolidement aſſuré ſa gloire.... par ces Eloges
ſi intereſſans, pleins d'une raiſon ſi fine et ſi pro-
fonde, qui font aimer et reſpecter les lettres, qui
inſpirent aux génies naiſſans la plus noble emulation, et qui feront paſſer le nom de l'auteur
à la poſterité, avec celui de la compagnie cé-
lebre dont il a été le digne organe, et des grands
hommes dont il s'eſt rendu l'egal en devenant leur
panégyriſte.

D'Alembert, Eloge de la Motte, p. 279.

NOTE XIII. VERSE 302.

No great Examples riſe, but many a Rule.] Before the appearance of Boſſu's celebrated treatiſe
on Epic poetry, the French had a ſimilar work
written in Latin. The learned Jeſuit Mambrun
publiſhed, in 1652, a quarto volume, entitled,
Diſſertatio Peripatetica de Epico Carmine. His
Diſſertation is founded on the principles of Ari-
ſtotle, whom he conſiders as infallible authority; and he introduces the Greek Philoſopher
to decide the following very curious queſtion,
which he argues with becoming gravity, Whether
the

the action of a woman can be sufficiently splendid to prove a proper subject for an Epic poem.— Having reasoned on this delicate point, with more learning than gallantry, he thus concludes the debate: Congruenter magis finem huic quæstioni ponere non licet, quam verbis Aristotelis capite 15 Poeticæ, ubi de moribus disputat, Δεύτερον δε, τα αρμοττοντα. Εστι γαρ ανδρειον μεν το ηθος, αλλ' ουκ αρμοττον γυναικι, το ανδρειαν η δεινην ειναι—id est, secunda proprietas morum est, ut sint congruentes, ut esse fortem mos est aliquis; at non congruit mulieri fortem esse aut terribilem ut vertit Riccobonus, vel *prudentem* ut Pacius. The latter interpetration of the word δεινην would render the decision of these Philosophers very severe indeed on the Female character, by supposing it incapable of displaying both fortitude and prudence.—The Fair Sex have found an advocate, on this occasion, in a French Epic Poet. The famous Chapelain, in the preface to his unfortunate Pucelle, has very warmly attacked these ungallant maxims of Mambrun and Aristotle. In speaking of certain critics, who had censured the choice of his subject, before the publication of his poem, he says, Ceux-cy, jurant sur le texte d'Aristote, maintiennent que la femme est une erreur de la nature, qui ayant toujours intention de

faire

faire un homme, s'arrefte fouvent en chemin, et fe voit contrainte, par la refiftance de la matiere, de laiffer fon deffein imparfait. Ils tiennent la force corporelle tellement neceffaire, dans la compofition d'un heros, que quand il n'y auroit autre defaut à reprocher à la femme, ils luy en refuferoient le nom, pour cela feulement, qu'elle n'a pas la vigueur d'un Athlete, et que la molleffe de fa complexion l'empefche de pouvoir durer au travail. Ils n'eftiment ce Sexe capable d'aucune penfée heroique, dans la creance que l'efprit fuit le temperament du corps, et que, dans le corps de la femme, l'efprit ne peut rien concevoir, qui ne fe fente de fa foibleffe. ——— Ces Meffieurs me pardonneront, toutefois, fi je leur dis qu'ils ne confiderent pas trop bien quelle eft la nature de la vertu heroique, qu'ils en definiffent l'effence, par un de fes moindres accidens, et qu'ils en font plutoft une vertu brutale, qu'une vertu divine. ——— Ils fe devroient fouvenir que cette vertu n'a prefque rien à faire avec le corps, et qu'elle confifte, non dans les efforts d'un Milon de Crotone, où l'efprit n'a aucune part, mais en ceux des ames nées pour les grandes chofes; quand par une ardeur plufqu' humaine, elles s'elevent audeffus d'elles-mefmes; qu'elles forment quelque deffein, dont l'utilité eft auffi grande que la difficulté, et qu'elles qu'elles choififfent les moyens de l'executer avec conftance et hauteur de courage. Pour prevenus qu'ils foient en faveurs des hommes, je ne penfe pas qu'ils vouluffent attribuer à leur ame un feul avantage, auquel l'ame de la femme ne puft afpirer, ni faire deux efpeces des deux fexes, defquels la raifon de tous les fages n'a fait qu'une jufqu'icy—je ne croy pas non plus qu'ils imaginent que les vertus morales ayent leur fiege ailleurs, que dans la volonté, ou dans l'entendement. Mais fi elles y ont leur fiege, et fi l'on ne peut dire que ces deux facultés foient autres, dans l'ame de la femme que dans l'ame de l'homme, ils ne peuvent, fans abfurdité, accorder une de ces vertus à l'homme, et ne l'accorder pas à la femme. En effet, cette belle penfée d'Ariftote qui a donné occafion à leur erreur, eft fi peu phyfique, qu'elle fait plus de tort à la philofophie du Lycée, qu'elle n'appuye l'opinion de ceux que nous combattons." Chapelain then enters into an hiftorical defence of Female dignity, and oppofes the authority of Plato to that of Ariftotle, concerning the propriety of women's ever appearing on the great theatre of active life. Happy had he fupported the Female caufe as forcibly, in the execution of his poem, as in the arguments of his preface: but Chapelain was unfortunately one of the many examples, which every

every country affords, that the moſt perfect union of virtue and erudition is utterly inſufficient to form a Poet; and, as he had the ill fate to be perſecuted by the pitileſs rigour of Boileau, his inharmonious poem can never ſink into a deſirable oblivion. The treatiſe of Mambrun ſeems to have excited, among the French, an eagerneſs to diſtinguiſh themſelves in the field of Epic poetry; for ſeveral Epic poems were publiſhed in France in a few years after that work appeared; but moſt of them, and particularly thoſe on ſcriptural ſubjects, were hardly ever known to exiſt.

> Le Jonas inconnu ſeche dans la pouſſiere,
> Le David imprimé n'a point vu la lumiere,
> Le Moïſe commence à moiſir par les bords.
> BOILEAU, Sat. ix.

The Alaric of Scudery, and the Clovis of Deſmareſts, can ſcarce be reckoned more fortunate; but in this band of unſucceſsful Epic writers, there was one Poet, of whom even the ſevere Boileau could not allow himſelf to ſpeak ill; this was Le Moine, the author of St. Louis. The Satiriſt being aſked, why he had never mentioned the poetry of Le Moine? replied with the two following verſes, parodied from Corneille,

Il s'eſt trop élevé pour en dire du mal,
Il s'eſt trop égaré pour en dire du bien.

The judicious and candid Heyne has beſtowed conſiderable applauſe on Le Moine, in one of his notes to the 6th book of Virgil, where he examines the different methods by which the Epic Poets have introduced their various pictures of futurity. From his account, Le Moine excels in this article.——Since the firſt publication of this eſſay, an obliging friend has favoured me with a copy of this neglected French poet, whom I had long ſought for in vain. To gratify the curious reader with a ſpecimen of this ſingular unequal bard, I ſhall inſert the paſſage ſo highly honoured by the applauſe of Heyne. I had thoughts of tranſlating it; but I find the character which Boileau gave of its author ſo completely juſt, that I deſpair of producing any adequate copy of the beauties and defects which are exhibited in the following lines. Let it ſuffice, therefore, to remark, that the 5th book of Saint Louis opens with a deſcription of the French army marching in order of battle towards Cairo. The Sultan is terrified, but conſoled by an offer of ſupernatural aſſiſtance from the enchanter Mireme. They ſally forth from the city together, in a magical car, which

is

is drawn by two demons; and the Poet proceeds thus:

Il fe voit pres de Caire, une plaine deferte,
Que d'un fable mouvant la nature a couverte;
Et qui femble une efpace applani fous les cieux,
Pour le feul exercice ou des vents ou des yeux.
Les pyramides font de cette vafte plaine,
Le fuperbe embarras & la montre hautaine,
Leur maffe offufque l'air, ofte l'efpace au jour,
Et l'œil fans repofer n'en peut faire le tour.
Les premiers feux du ciel a leurs pointes s'allument,
Et les feux de l'enfer fous leurs fondement fument.
La terre qui foutient tant de corps differens
Qui porte tant de bois, tant de monts fur fes flancs;
Ne fçauroit fans gêmir, porter de ces ftructures,
Les reftes fourcilleux & les hautes mazures.
Jadis pour les baftir les nations en corps,
Et les races par tout firent de grands efforts:
Il leur fallut fufpendre & tailler des montagnes,
Il leur fallut couvrir & combler des campagnes
Il fallut renverfer l'ordre des elemens,
Et de la terre en l'air, mettre les fondemens.
Auffi les nations & les races grevées
Perirent follement en ces vaines corvées.
Sous les pieds de ces monts taillez & fufpendus
Il s'étend des pays tenebreux & perdus,

Des deserts spacieux, des solitudes sombres,
Faites pour le sejour des morts & de leurs ombres,
Là sont les corps des roys & les corps des sultans,
Diversement rangez selon l'ordre des temps.
Les uns sont enchassez dans les creuses images,
A qui l'art a donné leur taille & leurs visages :
Et dans ces vains portraits, qui sont leurs monumens,
Leur orgueil se conserve avec leurs ossemens.
Les autres embaumez sont posez en des niches,
Où leurs ombres encore eclatantes & riches
Semble perpetuer malgré les loix du sort
La pompe de leur vie, en celle de leur mort.
De ce muet senat, de cette cour terrible,
Le silence epouvante, & la montre est horrible.
Là sont les devanciers joints à leurs descendans ;
Tous les regnes y sont ; on y voit tous les temps ;
Et cette antiquité si celebre en l'histoire,
Ces siecles si fameux par la voix de la gloire,
Reünis par la mort, en cette obscure nuit,
Y sont sans mouvement, sans lumiere & sans bruit.
Mireme dans ces lieux traitte avec les phantosmes,
Qui luy sont deputez des tenebreux royaumes :
Il y tient, loin du jour, dans un noir appareil,
Ses cercles infernaux, & son affreux conseil :
Il y fait ses concerts, & ses festes funebres ;
Et pour luy l'avenir ne luit qu'en ces tenebres.

Son

Son char à ce defert à peine fe rendit,
Que du fien auffi-toft le foleil defcendit ;
Et de peur de foüiller fes yeux & la lumiere,
D'un pas precipité terminant fa carriere,
Un broüillas fur fa route à la lune laiffa ;
La lune en eut horreur, & fon voile abaiffa.
L'Enchanteur fait un feu de fouffre & de refine,
Qui trouble plus les yeux, qu'il ne les illumine,
Et mene, à la vapeur de ce trifte flambeau,
Meledin qui le fuit, dans le fein du tombeau.
D'une baguette noire il compaffe un grand cerne :
Il fait de bruits confus refonner la caverne :
Et frappant d'un pied nud la terre par trois fois,
Pouffe jufqu'aux enfers cette effroyable voix.
Manes imperieux, ames jadis regnantes,
Jadis de ces grands corps fuperbes habitantes,
Si le foin de l'honneur avecque vous n'eft mort ;
Si pour luy, vous pouvez faire encor un effort ;
Si l'eternelle nuit qui l'enfer environne
Sur vos fronts a laiffé quelque ombre de couronne ;
Si pour voftre patrie il peut eftre refté,
A voftre fouvenir quelque fidelité ;
Sortez, efprits, fortez des royaumes funeftes,
De vos eftats bruflans venez fauver les reftes.
Vos thrônes, vos palais, vos tombeaux vont perir,
Si vous ne les venez au befoin fecourir.

Cette

Cette Egypte qui brufle & qui dès-ja fuccombe,
Voftre fiege autrefois, aujourd'huy voftre tombe,
Bientoft jufques à vous fa ruïne étendra ;
A vos os, à vos noms fa flame fe prendra :
De ce maudit ferpent, les œufs mal étouffez,
Bouffis de leur venin, de leur raye échauffez,
S'ils ne font écrafez, detruiront voftre race,
Et jufqu'à vos cercueils porteront leur audace.
L'Enchanteur à ces mots hautement prononcez
En joint de plus puiffans à voix baffe pouffez :
Et tout d'un temps, vomit de fa bouche qui fume
Le blafpheme & le fiel, les charmes & l'écume.
Cependant il s'éleve une obfcure vapeur,
De la terre qui tremble, & qui s'ouvre de peur :
Des manes grands & noirs y montent avec elle,
La troupe eft nombreufe & la fierté cruelle :
Cette vapeur leur fait comme un crefpe de ducil,
Et chacun d'eux fe range auprez de fon cercueil.
Leur demarche eft fuperbe & leur orgueil menace,
Au travers de leur voile ils montrent leur audace :
Ils font d'un air farouche, & d'un œil inhumain,
Ce qu'ils furent jadis du cœur & de la main :
Et n'ayant plus ny fer, ny flame, ny machine,
Ils font encor Tyrans du gefte & de la mine.
 Le premier qui parut, fut l'implacable roy
Qui par la nouveauté d'un edit plein d'effroy,

Aux

Aux enfans des Hebreux affigna la riviere,
Et pour berceau commun, & pour commune biere;
Et crût pouvoir, le temps & la mort avançant,
Perdre le peuple à naiftre avecque le naiffant.
Apres monta celuy, de qui l'ame endurcie
Fut tant de fois battuë & jamais adoucie ;
Ce Pharaon qui fut brifé de tous les fleaux,
Dont le ciel bat la terre, & dont il bat les eaux :
Et tout brifé qu'il fut, de fa penfée altiere,
L'enflure conferva jufques dans fa pouffiere.

 Apres les Pharaons, apres les autres roys,
Ennemis des Hebreux & de leurs faintes loix,
Monterent les tyrans, fectateurs des menfonges
De l'Arabe qui fit une loy de fes fonges.
Afame le cruel le premier y parut,
Déchiré du tourment dont jadis il mourut,
Lorfque du fang des faints, la voix aux cieux portée,
Sur fa tefte attira la juftice irritée.

 Le fecond fut Jezid, qui le premier voulut,
Dans l'Egypte abolir le figne de falut ;
Et par un facrilege énorme & fans exemple,
Sur la Croix eleva le Croiffant dans le temple.

 Abulmafen le fuit, encore dépité,
De la perte qu'il fit de la Sainte Cité,
Quand les Croifez vainqueurs de force l'emporterent,
Et pouffant leur victoire Antioche enleverent.

Son succeſſeur Tafur fait montre entre les morts,
Du teint noir que ſon ame apporta dans ſon corps.
Siracon qui le ſuit eſt fier de ſon audace,
Et plus fier d'avoir mis l'empire dans ſa race.
   Mais ſon fils Saladin de tout autre effaça
L'audace & la fierté, ſi toſt qu'il avança.
D'un rameau de laurier la feüille ſéche & noire
Sur ſon front conſervoit l'image de ſa gloire :
Sa mine eſtoit d'un brave & ſon geſte d'un grand ;
Son ombre avoit encor un air de conquerant :
Et ſembloit revenir, pour ſoûmettre à ſa lance
Ou les aigles de Rome, ou celles de Biſance.
Il ſe meſloit pourtant à ces geſtes d'orgueil,
Des ſignes de dépit, & des marques de dueil :
Et la fin de ſa race eteinte par ſon frere
De ſon ombre tiroit des regards de colere.
   L'eſprit de Saphadin rouge encore & taché
Du ſang de ſes neveux laſchement épanché,
A pas lents le ſuivoit, ſoit de honte, ou de crainte ;
Murmuroit à voix baſſe une confuſe plainte ;
Et du ſultan ſon fils prévoyant les malheurs,
Luy donnoit des ſoûpirs & des ombres de pleurs.
D'autres venus ſans ordre, accrurent l'aſſemblée :
La nuit en fut plus noire, elle en parut troublée :
Le ſeul Mireme ferme, en ce conſeil d'eſprits,
Ses charmes renouvelle & redouble ſes cris.

                                     Des

Des mains & de la bouche il leur fait violence :
Au gefte il joint la voix, & la voix au filence :
Il met tout en ufage, & pour dernier effort
Il prononce ces mots armez d'un nouveau fort.
 Ne parlez-vous point, opiniaftres ames !
Attendez-vous le fer, attendez-vous les flames !
Et toy, grand Saladin, le plus intereffé,
A fauver cet eftat que tes mains ont dreffé ;
Laifferas-tu tomber en pieces ton ouvrage ?
N'as-tu pour l'appuyer ny force ny courage ?
De cet efprit fi grand, de ce cœur fi hautain,
Il n'eft donc demeuré, qu'un fpectre pafle & vain,
Qu'un phantofme, qui n'a nul fentiment de gloire,
Qui laiffe ruiner fa tombe & fa memoire ?
Réveille, Saladin, réveille ces vertus,
Par lefquelles jadis les Croifez abbatus,
Ont fous toy tant de fois laiffé leurs Croix captives,
Et de leurs camps defaits ont engraiffé nos rives.
S'il n'eft plus temps, pour toy, de vaincre en bataillant,
Il fera toujours temps, de vaincre en confeillant.
 Saladin luy répond, d'une voix menaçante
Qui montra fa colere & la terreur augmente.
Le fang de mes neuf fils, par neuf crimes verfé,
A l'Egypt foüillée & le ciel offencé :
Et par arreft du ciel, jufqu'à me fatisfaire,
L'Egypt en doit porter la peine & ma colere :
            Ce

Ce fang, avec du fang, bien-toſt ſe lavera,
La race du meurtrier du throſne tombera ;
Et la pourpre qu'il a de ces crimes tachée,
Avec crime doit eſtre à ſon fils arrachée.
A cet arreſt fatal, porté pour m'appaiſer,
Meledin peut encore un remede oppoſer :
Il peut, en immolant, fils ou fille, à ma race,
De ſon mauvais deſtin détourner la menace :
Une mort ſeule peut payer pour tant de morts ;
Un membre retranché peut ſauver tout le corps.
Quand je l'auray permis, Mireme par ſes charmes,
Pourra de ſes demons mettre en œuvre les armes.
Le ſang de la victime à peine aura touché
Le grand fleuve, du ſang de mes enfans taché,
Que de tous ſes canaux, épandu ſur la terre,
Contre vos ennemis il portera la guerre.

Il finit, & ſuivy du terrible conſeil,
Qui ſentoit approcher le retour du ſoleil,
Dans la terre rentra, ne laiſſant que la crainte ;
A Meledin tremblant avec l'horreur empreinte.

The number of obſcure Epic writers in France is very trifling, compared to thoſe which Italy has produced ; the Italians have been indefatigable in this ſpecies of compoſition, and, as if they had reſolved to leave no Hero unſung, their celebrated

celebrated Novelist, Giraldi Cinthio, has written an Epic poem, in twenty-six cantos, on the exploits of Hercules.

NOTE XIV. VERSE 304.

Keen Boileau shall not want his proper praise.] Nicolas Boileau Despreaux was born *in* or *near* Paris, for it is a contested point, on the first of November 1636, and died in March 1711 of a dropsy, the very disease which terminated the life of his English rival. The Lutrin of Boileau, still considered by some French Critics of the present time as the best poem to which France has given birth, was first published in 1674. It is with great reason and justice that Voltaire confesses the Lutrin inferior to the Rape of the Lock. Few Poets can be so properly compared as Pope and Boileau; and, wherever their writings will admit of comparison, we may, without any national partiality, adjudge the superiority to the English Bard. These two great authors resembled each other as much in the integrity of their lives, as in the subjects and execution of their several compositions. There are two actions recorded of Boileau, which sufficiently prove that the inexorable Satirist had a

most

most generous and friendly heart; when Patru, the celebrated Advocate, who was ruined by his passion for literature, found himself under the painful necessity of selling his expensive library, and had almost agreed to part with it for a moderate sum, Boileau gave him a much superior price; and, after paying the money, added this condition to the purchase, that Patru should retain, during his life, the possession of the books. The succeeding instance of the Poet's generosity is yet nobler:—when it was rumoured at court that the King intended to retrench the pension of Corneille, Boileau hastened to Madame de Montespan, and said, that his Sovereign, equitable as he was, could not, without injustice, grant a pension to an author like himself, just ascending Parnassus, and take it from Corneille, who had so long been seated on the summit; that he entreated her, for the honour of the King, to prevail on his Majesty rather to strike off *his* pension, than to withdraw that reward from a man whose title to it was incomparably greater; and that he should more easily console himself under the loss of that distinction, than under the affliction of seeing it taken away from such a Poet as Corneille. This magnanimous application had the success which it deserved,

deserved, and it appears the more noble, when we recollect that the rival of Corneille was the intimate friend of Boileau.

The long and unreserved intercourse which subsisted between our Poet and Racine was highly beneficial and honourable to both. The dying farewell of the latter is the most expressive eulogy on the private character of Boileau: Je regarde comme un bonheur pour moi de mourir avant vous, said the tender Racine, in taking a final leave of his faithful and generous friend.

NOTE XV. VERSE 313.

Nor, gentle Gresset, shall thy sprightly rhyme.] This elegant and amiable writer was born at Amiens, and educated in the society of the Jesuits, to whom he has paid a grateful compliment in bidding them adieu. At the age of twenty-six he published his Ver-vert, a poem in four cantos, which commemorates

> La cause infortunée
> D'un Perroquet non moins brillant qu' Enée:
> Non moins dévot, plus malheureux que lui.

Voltaire has spoken invidiously of this delightful performance; but a spirited French Critic has very
justly

juſtly vindicated the merits of Greſſet in the following remark:—Le Ver-vert ſera toujours un poeme charmant et inimitable, ſans ſouiller ſa plume par l'impiété et la licence qui deſhonorent celle de l'auteur de *La Pucelle*, le Poete a ſu y répandre un agrément, une fraîcheur et une vivacité de coloris, qui le rendent auſſi piquant dans les détails, qu'il eſt riche et ingénieux dans la fiction. On placera toujours cet agreable badinage parmi les productions originales, propres à faire aimer des etrangers la gaieté Françoiſe en écartant toute mauvaiſe idée de nos mœurs.

NOTE XVI. VERSE 325.

See lovely Boccage, in ambition ſtrong.] Madame du Boccage is known to the Engliſh reader as the correſpondent of Lord Cheſterfield. This ingenious and ſpirited Lady has written three poems of the Epic kind—Le Paradis Terreſtre, in ſix cantos, from Milton; La Mort d'Abel, in five cantos, from Geſner; and a more original compoſition, in ten cantos, on the exploits of Columbus. I have alluded to a paſſage in the laſt poem, where Zama, the daughter of an Indian Chief, is thus deſcribed:

Comme

THIRD EPISTLE.

Comme Eve, elle etoit nue ; une egale innocence
L'offre aux regards fans honte, et voile fes appas ;
Les Graces qu'elle ignore accompagnent fes pas,
Et pour tout vêtement, en formant fa parure,
D'un plumage azuré couvrirent fa ceinture.

The works of this elegant female Poet contain an animated verfion of Pope's Temple of Fame. And fhe has added to her poetry an account of her travels through England, Holland, and Italy, in a feries of entertaining letters, addreffed to Madame du Perron, her fifter.

NOTE XVII. VERSE 344.

To fwell the glory of her great Voltaire.] Though the Henriade has been frequently reprinted, and the partizans of Voltaire have endeavoured to make it a national point of honour to fupport its reputation, it feems at length to be finking under that neglect and oblivion, which never fail to overtake every feeble offspring of the Epic Mufe. Several of our moft eminent Critics have attacked this performance with peculiar feverity, and fome have condemned it on the moft oppofite principles, merely becaufe it does not coincide with their re-

spective

spective systems. Their sentence has been passed only in short and incidental remarks; but a French writer, inflamed by personal animosity against Voltaire, has raised three octavo volumes on the defects of this single poem. Mr. Clement, in his "*En-tretiens sur le Poeme Epique relativement à la Henriade,*" has endeavoured to prove it utterly deficient in all the essential points of Epic poetry;—in the structure of its general plan, in the conduct of its various parts, in sentiment, in character, in style. His work indeed displays an acrimonious detestation of the Poet whom he examines; and perhaps there is hardly any human composition which could support the scrutiny of so rigid an inquisitor: the Henriade is utterly unequal to it; for in many articles we are obliged to confess, that the justice of the Critic is not inferior to his severity. He discovers, in his dissection of the Poem, the skill of an anatomist, with the malignity of an assassin. If any thing can deserve such rigorous treatment, it is certainly the artifice of Voltaire, who, in his Essay on Epic Poetry, has attempted, with much ingenuity, to sink the reputation of all the great Epic Writers, that he might raise himself to their level; an attempt in which no author can ultimately succeed; for, as D'Alembert has admirably

THIRD EPISTLE.

rably remarked on a different occasion, Le public laissera l'amour propre de chaque ecrivain faire son plaidoyer, rira de leurs efforts, non de genie, mais de raisonnement, pour hausser leur place, et finira par mettre chacun à la sienne.

NOTE XVIII. VERSE 475.

And, shrouded in a mist of moral spleen.] It seems to be the peculiar infelicity of Pope, that his moral virtues have had a tendency to diminish his poetical reputation. Possessing a benevolent spirit, and wishing to make the art to which he devoted his life, as serviceable as he could to the great interests of mankind, he soon quitted the higher regions of poetry, for the more level, and more frequented field of Ethics and of Satire. He declares, with a noble pride arising from the probity of his intention,

That not in Fancy's maze he wander'd long,
But stoop'd to truth, and moraliz'd his song.

The severity of Criticism has from hence inferred, that his imagination was inferior to the other faculties of his mind, and that he possessed not that
vigour

vigour of genius which might enable him to rank with our more sublime and pathetic Bards. This inference appears to me extremely defective both in candour and in reason; it would surely be more generous, and I will venture to add, more just, to assign very different causes for his having latterly applied himself to moral and satyric composition. If his preceding poems displayed only a moderate portion of fancy and of tenderness, we might indeed very fairly conjecture, that he quitted the kind of poetry, where these qualities are particularly required, because Nature directed him to shine only as the Poet of reason.—But his earlier productions will authorize an opposite conclusion. At an age when few authors have produced any capital work, Pope gave the world two poems, one the offspring of imagination, and the other of sensibility, which will ever stand at the head of the two poetical classes to which they belong: his Rape of the Lock, and his Eloise, have nothing to fear from any rivals, either of past or of future time. When a writer has displayed such early proofs of exquisite fancy, and of tender enthusiasm, those great constituents of the real Poet, ought we not to regret that he did not give a greater scope and freer exercise to these qualities, rather than to assert that he did

did not poſſeſs them in a ſuperlative degree?—Why then, it may be aſked, did he confine himſelf to compoſitions in which theſe have little ſhare? The life and character of Pope will perfectly explain the reaſons, why he did not always follow the higher ſuggeſtions of his own natural genius. He had entertained an opinion, that by ſtooping to truth, and employing his talents on the vices and follies of the paſſing time, he ſhould be moſt able to benefit mankind. The idea was perhaps ill-founded, but his conduct in conſequence of it was certainly noble. Its effects however were moſt unhappy; for it took from him all his enjoyment of life, and may injure, in ſome degree, his immortal reputation: by ſuffering his thoughts to dwell too much on knaves and fools, he fell into the ſplenetic deluſion, that the world is nothing but a compound of vice and folly; and from hence he has been reproached for ſuppoſing that all human merit was confined to himſelf, and to a few of his moſt intimate correſpondents.

There was an amiable peculiarity in the character of Pope, which had great influence both on his conduct and compoſition—he embraced the ſentiments of thoſe he loved with a kind of ſuperſtitious regard; his imagination and his judgment were

were perpetually the dupes of an affectionate heart: it was this which led him, at the requeſt of his idol Bolingbroke, to write a ſublime poem on metaphyſical ideas which he did not perfectly comprehend; it was this which urged him almoſt to quarrel with Mr. Allen, in compliance with the caprices of a female friend; it was this which induced him, in the warmth of gratitude, to follow the abſurd hints of Warburton with all the blindneſs of infatuated affection. Whoever examines the life and writings of Pope with a minute and unprejudiced attention, will find that his excellencies, both as a Poet and a Man, were peculiarly his own; and that his failings were chiefly owing to the ill judgment, or the artifice, of his real and pretended friends. The laviſh applauſe and the advice of his favourite Atterbury, were perhaps the cauſe of his preſerving the famous character of Addiſon, which, finely written as it is, all the lovers of Pope muſt wiſh him to have ſuppreſſed. Few of his friends had ntegrity or frankneſs ſufficient to perſuade him, that his ſatires would deſtroy the tranquillity of his life, and cloud the luſtre of his fame: yet, to the honour of Lyttelton, be it remembered, that he ſuggeſted ſuch ideas to the Poet, in the verſes
which

which he wrote to him from Rome, with all the becoming zeal of enlightened friendship:

No more let meaner Satire dim the rays
That flow majestic from thy nobler bays!
In all the flowery paths of Pindus stray,
But shun that thorny, that unpleasing way!
Nor, when each soft, engaging Muse is thine,
Address the least attractive of the Nine!

This generous admonition did not indeed produce its intended effect, for other counsellors had given a different bias to the mind of the Poet, and the malignity of his enemies had exasperated his temper; yet he afterwards turned his thoughts towards the composition of a national Epic poem, and possibly in consequence of the hint which this Epistle of Lyttelton contains. The intention was formed too late, for it arose in his decline of life. Had he possessed health and leisure to execute such a work, I am persuaded it would have proved a glorious acquisition to the literature of our country: the subject indeed which he had chosen must be allowed to have an unpromising appearance; but the opinion of Addison concerning his Sylphs, which was surely honest, and not invidious, may teach

teach us hardly ever to decide againſt the intended works of a ſuperior genius. Yet in all the Arts we are perpetually tempted to pronounce ſuch deciſions. I have frequently condemned ſubjects which my friend Romney had ſelected for the pencil; but in the ſequel, my opinion only proved that I was near-ſighted in thoſe regions of imagination, where his keener eyes commanded all the proſpect.

NOTES

TO THE

FOURTH EPISTLE.

NOTE I. VERSE 103.

PROCEED, ye Sisters of the tuneful Shell.] For the advice which I have thus ventured to give such of my fair readers as have a talent for poetry, I shall produce them a much higher poetical authority. In the age of Petrarch, an Italian Lady, named Giustina Perrot, was desirous of distinguishing herself by this pleasing accomplishment; but the remarks of the world, which represented it

as improper for her sex, discouraged her so far, that she was almost tempted to relinquish her favourite pursuit. In her doubts on this point, she consulted the celebrated Poet of her country, in an
elegant

IO vorrei pur drizzar queste mie piume
   Colà, Signor, dove il desio n'invita,
E dopo morte rimaner' in vita
Col chiaro di virtute inclyto lume
Ma' volgo inerte, che dal rio costume
Vinto, ha d' ogni suo ben la via smarrita,
Come degna di biasmo ogn' hor m' addita
Ch' ir tenti d' Elicona al sacro fiume.
All' ago, al fuso, piu ch' al lauro, o al mirto,
Come che qui non sia la gloria mia,
Vuol ch' habbia sempre questa mente intesa.
Dimmi tu hormai, che per piu dritta via
A Parnasso t' en vai, nobile spirto,
Dovrò dunque lasciar sì degna impresa?

elegant Sonnet; and received his anfwer on the interefting fubject in the fame poetical form. I fhall add the two Sonnets, with an imitation of each;

THE SONNET OF GIUSTINA TO PETRARCH.

GLADLY would I exchange inglorious eafe
    For future fame, the Poet's fond defire!
And ftill to live, in fpite of death, afpire
By Virtue's light, that darknefs cannot feize:
But, ftupified, by Cuftom's blank decrees,
The idle vulgar, void of liberal fire,
Bid me, with fcorn, from Helicon retire,
And rudely blame my generous hope to pleafe.
Diftaffs, not laurels, to your fex belong,
They cry—as honour were beyond our view;
To fuch low cares they wifh my fpirit bent.
Say thou! who marcheft, mid the favour'd few,
To high Parnaffus, with triumphant fong,
Should I abandon fuch a fair intent?

LA gola, e 'l fonno, e l' oziofe piume
    Hanno del mondo ogni virtù fbandita,
Ond' è dal corfo fuo quafi fmarrita
Noftra natura vinta dal coftume :
Ed è fi fpento ogni benigno lume
Del ciel, per cui s' informa umana vita,
Che per cofa mirabile s' addita
Chi vuol far d' Elicona nafcer fiume.
Qual vaghezza di lauro, qual di mirto?
Povera e nuda vai filofofia,
Dice la turba al vil guadagno intefa.
Pochi compagni avrai per l'altra via
Tanto ti prego più, gentile fpirto,
Non lafciar la magnanima tua imprefa!

NOTE II. VERSE 210.

As wounded Learning blushes to recite!] Milton fold the copy of Paradife Loft for the fum of five pounds, on the condition of receiving fifteen pounds

FOURTH EPISTLE.

THE ANSWER OF PETRARCH.

LUXURIOUS pleasure, and lethargic ease,
   Have deaden'd in the world each bright desire:
Our thoughts no more with Nature's force aspire;
Custom's cold powers the drooping fancy seize:
So lost each light that taught the soul to please,
Each heavenly spark of life-directing fire,
That all, who join the Heliconian choir,
Are frantic deem'd by Folly's dull decrees.
What charms, what worth to Laurel-wreaths be-
   long?
Naked and poor Philosophy we view,
Exclaims the crowd, on sordid gain intent.—
Associates in thy path thou'lt find but few;
The more I pray thee, Nymph of graceful song,
Indulge thy spirit in its noble bent!

---

pounds more at three subsequent periods, to be regulated by the sale of the Poem.—For the ceiling at Whitehall, Rubens received three thousand pounds.

NOTE

NOTE III. VERSE 298.

Receive the Laurel from Imperial Charles!] Ariosto is said to have been publicly crowned with laurel at Mantua, by the Emperor Charles the Vth, towards the end of the year 1532. This fact has been disputed by various writers, but it seems to be sufficiently established by the researches of Mazzuchelli.

The custom of crowning Poets with laurel is almost as ancient as poetry itself, says the Abbé du Resnel, in his Recherches sur les Poetes couronnez, a work which contains but scanty information on this curious topic. Petrarch is generally supposed to have revived this ancient solemnity, which had been abolished as a pagan institution in the reign of the Emperor Theodosius. It appears however, from two passages in the writings of Boccacio, that Dante had entertained serious thoughts of this honourable distinction, which his exile precluded him from receiving, as he chose, says his Biographer, to be crowned only in his native city.

An amusing volume might be written on the honours which have been paid to Poets in different ages, and in various parts of the world. It is remarkable, that the most unpolished nations have been the most lavish in rewarding their Bards.
There

FOURTH EPISTLE.

There are two instances on record, in which poetical talents have raised their possessors even to sovereign dominion. The Scythians chose the Poet Thamyris for their king, though he was not a native of their country, επι τοσητον ηκε κιθαρωδιας, ως και βασιλεα σφων, καιπερ επηλυτον οντα, Σκυθας ποιησασθαι. Hist. Poet. Script. Edit. Gale, p. 250. Saxo Grammaticus begins the sixth book of his History by relating, that the Danes bestowed their vacant diadem on the Poet Hiarnus, as a reward for his having composed the best epitaph on their deceased sovereign Frotho. From the four Latin verses which the Historian has given us, as a translation of this extraordinary epitaph, we may venture to affirm, that the poetical monarch obtained his crown on very easy conditions.

NOTE IV. VERSE 314.

For him her fountains gush with golden streams.] Of the great wealth which flowed into the hands of this extraordinary Poet, his friend and biographer Montalvan has given a particular account. This author concludes that Lope de Vega gained by his dramatic works alone a sum nearly equal to 20,000 pounds sterling; the revenue arising from the posts he held, and from his pension, was very considerable.

confiderable. His opulence was much encreased by the moft fplendid inftances of private liberality. He received many coftly prefents from various characters to whom he was perfonally unknown; and he was himfelf heard to fay, in fpeaking of his generous patron, that the Duke of Seffa alone had given him, at different periods of his life, fums almoft amounting to fix thoufand pounds.

It muft be confeffed, that the noble patrons of Englifh poetry have not equalled this example of Spanifh munificence, even if we admit the truth of our traditionary anecdotes concerning the generofity of Lord Southampton to Shakefpeare, and of Sir Philip Sidney to Spenfer. Confidering the liberality for which our nation is fo juftly celebrated, it is remarkable, that not a fingle Englifh Poet appears to have been enriched by our monarchs: yet Spenfer had every claim to the bounty of Elizabeth; he fung her praifes in a ftrain which might gratify her pride; and of all who have flattered the great, he may juftly be confidered as the moft worthy of reward. His fong was the tribute of his heart as well as of his fancy, and the fex of his idol may be faid to purify his incenfe from all the offenfive particles of fervile adulation. The neglect which he experienced from the vain, imperious, and ungrateful Elizabeth, appears the

more

more striking, when we recollect, that her lovely rival, the beautiful and unfortunate Queen of Scots, signalized her superior generosity by a magnificent present of plate to the French Poet Ronsard. This neglected Bard was once the darling of France, and perhaps equalled Lope de Vega in the honours which he received: his sovereign, Charles the Ninth, composed some elegant verses in his praise, and the city of Toulouse presented him with a Minerva of massive silver.

If our princes and nobles have not equalled those of other kingdoms in liberality to the great Poets of their country, England may yet boast the name of a private gentleman, who discovered in this respect a most princely spirit; no nation, either ancient or modern, can produce an example of munificence more truly noble than the annual gratuity which Akenside received from Mr. Dyson; a tribute of generous and affectionate admiration, endeared to its worthy possessor by every consideration which could make it honourable both to himself and to his patron!

It has been lately lamented by an elegant and accomplished writer, who had too much reason for the complaint, that " the profession of Literature, " by far the most laborious of any, leads to no " real benefit." Experience undoubtedly proves that it has a general tendency to impoverish its votaries; and the legiflators of every country would act perhaps a wife, at all events an honourable part, if they corrected this tendency, by eftablifhing public emoluments for fuch as eminently diftinguifh themfelves in the various branches of fcience. It is furely poffible to form fuch an eftablifhment, which, without proving a national burthen, might aggrandize the literary glory of the nation, by preferving her men of letters from the evils fo frequently connected with their purfuits, by fecuring, to thofe who deferve it, the poffeffion of eafe and honour, without damping their emulation, or deftroying their independence.

NOTES

NOTES

TO THE

FIFTH EPISTLE.

NOTE I.   VERSE 76.

THE loose Petronius gave the maxim birth.] Aristotle has said but little, in his Poetics, concerning that weighty point, which has so much employed and embarrassed the modern Critics—the machinery of the Epic poem; and the little which he has said might rather furnish an argument for its exclusion, than justify its use. But Rome, in her most degenerate days, produced a writer, to whose authority, contemptible as it is, most frequent appeals have been made in this curious literary queftion. In almoft every modern author who has touched, however flightly, on Epic poetry, we may find at leaft fome part of the following fentence from Petronius Arbiter :—Ecce, belli civilis ingens opus quifquis attigerit, nifi plenus litteris, fub onere labetur. Non enim res geftæ verfibus comprehendendæ funt, quod longe melius, hiftorici faciunt; fed per ambages, deorumque minifteria, & fabulofum fententiarum tormentum præcipitandus eft liber fpiritus ; ut potius furentis animi vaticinatio appareat, quam religiofæ orationis fub teftibus fides.

Thefe remarks on the neceffity of celeftial agents, were evidently made to depreciate the Pharfalia of Lucan; and Petronius may be called a fair Critic, as Pope faid of Milbourne, on his oppofition to Dryden, becaufe he produces his own poetry in contraft to that which he condemns. His fpecimen of the manner in which he thought an Epic poem fhould be conducted, fufficiently proves the abfurdity of his criticifm ; for how infipid is the fable in thofe verfes which he has oppofed to the Pharfalia, when compared to the firft book of Lucan! Yet the Epic compofition of Petronius has not wanted admirers : a Dutch Commentator is bold enough to fay, that he prefers this fingle rhapfody to three hundred volumes of fuch poetry as
                                                Lucan's:

Lucan's: an opinion which can only lead us to exclaim with Boileau,

Un fot trouve toujours un plus fot qui l'admire.

If men of letters, in the age of Lucan, differed in their sentiments concerning machinery, the great changes that have since happened in the world, and the disquisitions which have appeared on the subject, are very far from having reconciled the judgment of modern writers on this important article. Two eminent Critics of the present time have delivered opinions on this topic so singularly opposite to each other, that I shall transcribe them both.

" In a theatrical entertainment, which employs
" both the eye and the ear, it would be a grofs
" abfurdity to introduce upon the stage superior
" Beings in a visible shape. There is not place for
" such objection in an Epic poem; and Boileau,
" with many other Critics, declares strongly for
" that sort of machinery in an Epic poem. But
" waving authority, which is apt to impose upon
" the judgment, let us draw what light we can
" from reason. I begin with a preliminary re-
" mark, that this matter is but indistinctly han-

" dled by Critics. The poetical privilege of ani-
" mating infenfible objects for enlivening a defcrip-
" tion, is very different from what is termed *ma-*
" *chinery*, where deities, angels, devils, or other
" fupernatural powers, are introduced as real per-
" fonages, mixing in the action, and contributing
" to the cataftrophe; and yet thefe two things
" are conftantly jumbled together in the reafon-
" ing. The former is founded on a natural princi-
" ple; but can the latter claim the fame autho-
" rity? So far from it, that nothing is more unna-
" tural. Its effects at the fame time are deplora-
" ble. Firft, it gives an air of fiction to the whole,
" and prevents that impreffion of reality which is
" requifite to intereft our affections, and to move
" our paffions; which of itfelf is fufficient to
" explode machinery, whatever entertainment it
" may afford to readers of a fantaftic tafte or irre-
" gular imagination. And next, were it poffible,
" by difguifing the fiction, to delude us into a
" notion of reality, which I think can hardly be,
" an infuperable objection would ftill remain,
" which is, that the aim or end of an Epic poem
" can never be attained in any perfection where
" machinery is introduced; for an evident reafon,
" that virtuous emotions cannot be raifed fuccefs-
" fully, but by the actions of thofe who are en-

" dued

FIFTH EPISTLE.

" dued with paffions and affections like our own,
" that is, by human actions: and as for moral in-
" struction, it is clear that none can be drawn from
" Beings who act not upon the fame principles
" with us. Homer, it is true, introduces the Gods
" into his fable; but the religion of his country
" authorized that liberty; it being an article in
" the Grecian creed, that the Gods often interpofe
" vifibly and bodily in human affairs. I muft,
" however, obferve, that Homer's Deities do no
" honour to his poems. Fictions that tranfgrefs
" the bounds of nature feldom have a good effect;
" they may inflame the imagination for a moment,
" but will not be relifhed by any perfon of a cor-
" rect tafte. They may be of fome ufe to the lower
" rank of writers; but an author of genius has
" much finer materials of nature's production
" for elevating his fubject, and making it intereft-
" ing.——Voltaire, in his Effay upon Epic Poe-
" try, talking of the Pharfalia, obferves judiciouf-
" ly, that the proximity of time, the notoriety
" of events, the character of the age, enlightened
" and political, joined with the folidity of Lucan's
" fubject, deprived him of all liberty of poetical
" fiction. Is it not amazing, that a Critic who
" reafons fo juftly with refpect to others, can be fo

" blind

" blind with respect to himself? Voltaire, not sa-
" tisfied to enrich his language with images drawn
" from invisible and superior Beings, introduces
" them into the action. In the sixth canto of the
" Henriade, St. Louis appears in person, and ter-
" rifies the soldiers; in the seventh canto, St.
" Louis sends the God of Sleep to Henry; and in
" the tenth, the demons of Discord, Fanaticism,
" War, &c. assist Aumale in a single combat with
" Turenne, and are driven away by a good angel
" brandishing the sword of God. To blend such
" fictitious personages in the same action with
" mortals, makes a bad figure at any rate, and
" is intolerable in a history so recent as that of
" Henry IV. This singly is sufficient to make the
" Henriade a short-lived poem, were it otherwise
" possessed of every beauty."—*Elements of Criticism,*
vol. ii. p. 389, 4th edition.

" The Pagan Gods and Gothic Fairies were
" equally out of credit when Milton wrote. He
" did well therefore to supply their room with An-
" gels and Devils. If these too should wear out of
" the popular creed (and they seem in a hopeful
" way, from the liberty some late Critics have
" taken with them) I know not what other expe-
                                            " dients

FIFTH EPISTLE.

"dients the Epic Poet might have recourse to; but
"this I know—the Pomp of verse, the energy of
"description, and even the finest moral paintings,
"would stand him in no stead. Without *admira-*
"*tion* (which cannot be effected but by the mar-
"vellous of celestial intervention, I mean the
"agency of superior natures really existing, or by
"the illusion of the fancy taken to be so) no Epic
"poem can be long-lived. I am not afraid to
"instance in the Henriade itself, which, notwith-
"standing the elegance of the composition, will
"in a short time be no more read than the
"Gondibert of Sir W. Davenant, and for the
"same reason."—*Letters on Chivalry and Ro-*
mance, Letter X.

I have thus ventured to confront these eminent
critical antagonists, that, while they engage and
overthrow each other, we may observe the injustice
produced by the spirit of systematical criticism, even
in authors most respectable for their talents and
erudition.—Here is the unfortunate Voltaire placed
between two critical fires, which equally destroy
him. The *first* Critic asserts that the Henriade
must be short-lived, because the Poet *has introduced invisible and superior agents*;—the *second*
denounces the same fate against it, because *it wants*
the

the *agency of superior natures:* yet surely every reader of Poetry, who is not influenced by any particular syftem, will readily allow, that if Voltaire had treated his fubject with true Epic fpirit in all other points, neither the introduction nor the abfence of St. Louis could be fingly fufficient to plunge the Henriade in oblivion. Indeed the learned author, who has fpoken in fo peremptory a manner concerning the neceffity of fupernatural agents to preferve the exiftence of an Epic poem, appears rather unfortunate in the two examples by which he endeavours to fupport his doctrine; for the Epic poems both of Davenant and Voltaire have fufficient defects to account for any neglect which may be their lot, without confidering the article of Machinery.

If I have warmly oppofed any decifions of this exalted Critic, it is from a perfuafion (in which I may perhaps be miftaken) that *fome* of his maxims have a ftrong tendency to injure an art highly dear to us both; an art on which his genius and learning have caft *many* rays of pleafing and of ufeful light.

NOTE

NOTE II. VERSE 166.

But howling dogs the fancied Orpheus tore.] This acecdote of Neanthus, the son of King Pittacus, is related by Lucian. The curious reader may find it in the second volume of Dr. Francklin's spirited translation of that lively author, page 355 of the quarto edition.

NOTE III. VERSE 276.

And spotless Laurels in that field be won.] The Indian mythology, as it has lately been illustrated in the writings of Mr. Holwell, is finely calculated to answer the purpose of any poetical genius who may wish to introduce new machinery into the serious Epic Poem. Besides the powerful charm of novelty, it would have the advantage of not clashing with our national religion; for the endeavours of Mr. Holwell to reconcile the ancient and pure doctrine of Bramah with the dispensation of Christ, have so far succeeded, that if his system does not satisfy a theologist, it certainly affords a sufficient basis for the structure of a Poem. In perusing his account of the Indian scripture, every reader of
imagination

imagination may, I think, perceive, that the Shaftah might fupply a poetical fpirit with as rich a mafs of ideal treafure as fancy could wifh to work upon.—An Epic Poet, defirous of laying the fcene of his action in India, would be more embarraffed to find interefting Heroes than proper Divinities.—Had juftice and generofity infpired and guided that Englifh valour, which has fignalized itfelf on the plains of Indoftan; had the arms of our country been employed to deliver the native Indians from the oppreffive ufurpation of the Mahometan powers; fuch exploits would prefent to the Epic Mufe a fubject truly noble, and the mythology of the Eaft might enrich it with the moft fplendid decorations. Whether it be poffible or not to find fuch a fubject in the records of our Indian hiftory, I leave the reader to determine.—Our great Hiftorian of the Roman empire has intimated, in a note to the firft volume of his immortal work, that " the wonderful expedition of Odin, " which deduces the enmity of the Goths and Ro- " mans from fo memorable a caufe, might fupply the " noble ground-work of an Epic poem." The idea is certainly both juft and fplendid. Had Gray been ever tempted to engage in fuch a work, he would probably have convinced us, that the Northern mythology has ftill fufficient power to feize and enchant

chant the imagination, as much in Epic as in Lyric composition.

It may amuse our speculative Critics, to consider how far the *religious Gothic fables* should be introduced or rejected, to render such a performance most interesting to a modern reader. Few judges would agree in their sentiments on the question; and perhaps the great dispute concerning Machinery cannot be fairly adjusted, till some happy genius shall possess ambition and perseverance enough to execute two Epic poems, in the one adopting, and in the other rejecting, supernatural agents; for Reason alone is by no means an infallible conductor in the province of Fancy; and in the poetical as well as the philosophical world, experiment is the surest guide to truth.

END OF THE FOURTH VOLUME.

www.ingramcontent.com/pod-product-compliance
Lightning Source LLC
Chambersburg PA
CBHW031752230426
43669CB00007B/589